Leckie × Leckie
Scotland's leading educational publishers
Helping students achieve success for 2…

1989–2009

Dear Principal Teacher

General/Credit Computing: Practice Pa…
Special offer – discount prices

These important new resources include completely new prac… …with fully worked answers, available for the first time and designed for use in t… …classroom and at home. I have pleasure in enclosing free of charge copies for your inspection.

Competitively priced at £5.99, **Practice Papers for SQA Exams** have been produced following extensive market research amongst teachers. They feature:

- **Fully worked answer sections** to support learning by showing the student not just the answer but how to reach it: highly effective as a teaching resource!
- Marking schemes that allow you to see how marks are allocated
- Designed to look and feel just like an SQA exam paper to mirror the exam experience
- Packed full of practical exam revision hints and tips
- Keen pricing and with fantastic discounts available to help stretch your school budget!
- Choose whether to complete a whole paper or let the handy topic index allow you to focus on specific subjects
- Unlimited lifespan as papers are not year-dependent

Leckie & Leckie is pleased to offer you up to a massive 35% discount - yes, that's a **35% discount!** – off bulk purchases of all **Practice Papers for SQA Exams.** Take a look at the enclosed order form for more details of how to order at these special discount prices!

Now is the perfect time to top up your stock of revision resources by taking advantage of our special offer on this major new series. But hurry – to ensure you're eligible for these introductory discounts, ***we must receive your order by 11th September 2009***.

GET YOUR FREE PDF FOR WHITEBOARD USE NOW!

Order more than 20 copies of any title and you'll receive a PDF version of this title absolutely free of charge. Perfect for whiteboard use in class so that you get even more value from your classroom set!

For more information please call me on 01560 482592 (office) or 07734 331250 (mobile); alternatively, our dedicated Customer Services Team on 0870 460 7662 will be happy to answer any queries.

Yours faithfully

Valerie Henderson

Valerie Henderson
Schools Consultant
14 Cutsburn Road, Stewarton, KA3 5PD
Tel/Fax: 01560 482592 Mobile: 07734 331250
Email: valerie.henderson@leckieandleckie.co.uk

Leckie & Leckie Ltd
Registered in Scotland under Company number SC198254
Registered Office : Western Part of Frederick, 4 Queen Street, Edinburgh, EH2 1JE
Tel: +44 (0)131 220 6831 Fax: +44 (0)131 225 9987 Email enquiries@leckieandleckie.co.uk Website: www.leckieandleckie.co.uk

Leckie × Leckie
Scotland's leading educational publishers

ANNOUNCING A MAJOR NEW SERIES TO HELP STUDENTS PREPARE FOR SQA EXAMINATIONS

PRACTICE PAPERS FOR SQA EXAMS

Featuring fully worked answer sections, exam tips and advice

From 25% off!
Order a total of 100 copies before 11th September to claim 35% discount!

Special September discounts!

General Credit Computing
Author: Richard Ellis

Higher Computing
Author: Ted Hastings

Extent: c.112 pp Format: A4
AVAILABLE FROM JULY 2009

Discount structure:
Our discount structure is based on how many copies you order.

Copies	Discount	Price
1-19	25%	£4.49
20-99	30%	£4.19
100+	35%	£3.89

FREE PDF versions available for whiteboard use*

KEY FEATURES

- Completely new practice papers from Leckie & Leckie, available for the first time
- Produced following extensive market research amongst teachers
- Ready for the beginning of the autumn term – get started with exam practice on the first day of Back to School!
- Featuring fully worked answer sections to support learning by showing the student not just the answer but how to reach it: highly effective as a teaching resource
- Marking schemes allow you to see how marks are allocated, which helps plan time during the exam
- Highly effective for use in class and for revision at home
- Designed to look and feel just like an SQA exam paper to mirror the exam experience
- Packed full of practical exam hints and tips
- Choose whether to complete a whole paper or let the handy topic index allow you to focus on specific subjects
- The perfect tool for students wanting to practise exams questions and understand how to achieve the very best grade
- Unlimited lifespan as papers are not year-dependent
- Competitively priced and with discounts available to help stretch your budget!
- *This applies to orders of 20+ copies. Please call 0131 220 6831 or email enquiries@leckieandleckie.co.uk for further details

Please turn over to order your inspection copies today!

Practice makes Perfect!

HOW TO ORDER

Special September discounts!

Please contact our Customer Services team:

By phone: 0870 460 7662
By fax: 0870 787 1720
By email: leckieandleckie@harpercollins.co.uk

By post. Tick the boxes below and send this form to: Leckie Educational, Customer Services Department, HarperCollins, Campsie View, Westerhill Road, Bishopbriggs, Glasgow G64 2QT

TITLE	ISBN	Price for 1-19 copies	Price for 20-99 copies	Price for 100+ copies	Qty	Amount
Standard Grade General / Credit Computing Practice Papers for SQA Exams NEW July 2009	9781843727675	£4.49	£4.19	£3.89		
Higher Computing Practice Papers for SQA Exams NEW August 2009	9781843727866	£4.49	£4.19	£3.89		
	P&P					£5.95
ORDER A TOTAL OF 100 COPIES BEFORE 11TH SEPTEMBER TO GET 35% OFF	TOTAL					

YOUR DETAILS	
Name	
Email	
Position	
School/College	
Address	
Postcode	
Telephone number	
Date	

For further information please contact Valerie Henderson:
Direct dial: 01560 482592 or email valerie.henderson@leckieandleckie.co.uk

We store your data to ensure that you are kept fully informed of our products and services.
Your data is protected and not passed on to third parties. If you do not wish to receive further information from companies within Huveaux PLC, please tick this box ☐
While every effort has been made to ensure that prices are correct at time of going to print, Leckie & Leckie reserves the right to change these prices without notification.

Leckie × Leckie
Scotland's leading educational publishers

Practice Papers for SQA Exams

Standard Grade | General | Credit

Computing Studies

01/150609

ISBN 978-1-84372-767-5

Published by
Leckie & Leckie Ltd, 4 Queen Street, Edinburgh, EH2 1JE
Tel: 0131 220 6831 Fax: 0131 225 9987
enquiries@leckieandleckie.co.uk www.leckieandleckie.co.uk

A CIP Catalogue record for this book is available from the British Library.

Leckie & Leckie Ltd is a division of Huveaux plc.

Questions and answers in this book do not emanate from SQA. All of our entirely new and original Practice Papers have been written by experienced authors working directly for the publisher.

Introduction

Layout of the Book

This book contains practice exam papers, which mirror the actual SQA exam as much as possible. The layout, paper colour and question level are all similar to the actual exam that you will sit, so that you are familiar with what the exam paper will look like.

The answer section is at the back of the book. Each answer contains a worked out answer or solution so that you can see how the right answer has been arrived at. The answers also include practical tips on how to tackle certain types of questions, details of how marks are awarded and advice on just what the examiners will be looking for.

Revision advice is provided in this introductory section of the book, so please read on!

How To Use This Book

The Practice Papers can be used in two main ways:

1. You can complete an entire practice paper as preparation for the final exam. If you would like to use the book in this way, you can either complete the practice paper under exam style conditions by setting yourself a time for each paper and answering it as well as possible without using any references or notes. Alternatively, you can answer the practice paper questions as a revision exercise, using your notes to produce a model answer. Your teacher may mark these for you.
2. You can use the Topic Index at the front of this book to find all the questions within the book that deal with a specific topic. This allows you to focus specifically on areas that you particularly want to revise or, if you are mid-way through your course, it lets you practise answering exam-style questions for just those topics that you have studied.

The Exam

Syllabus

Listed below is an outline of the topics assessed in the Standard Grade Computing exams. The Credit and the General course cover the same topics but, at Credit level, the topic is done in more depth and the exam questions are more demanding.

You can obtain a detailed syllabus from the SQA website at www.sqa.org.uk or ask your teacher for a copy.

Computer Applications

General Purpose Packages
Word Processing
Spreadsheets
Databases
Graphics
Desk Top Publishing
Presentation and Multimedia
Web Page Creation
Expert Systems

Communications and Networks

Electronic Communication
LANs and WANs
Internet

Industrial and Commercial Applications

Commercial Data Processing
Industrial Applications / Automated Systems

Computer Systems

Hardware
System Software
Operating Systems
Low Level Machine

Time

The time allocations for the exam are different for the Foundation, General and Credit exams.

Level	Time
Foundation	1 hour
General	1 hour 15 min
Credit	1 hour 45 min

Be aware of the time as you proceed through the exam.

For example, if you are half way through a Credit exam after 20 minutes, then you are almost certainly not giving enough full and detailed answers. On the other hand, you do not want to get in a position where you are rushing to finish the last few questions and give messy and incomplete answers towards the end of the paper. Take care to pace yourself sensibly and avoid both of these two extremes.

Every year thousands of candidates leave the exam early. This can never be a good thing to do in an exam like computing where an answer can always be improved or the steps in a calculation checked over for silly mistakes. Look out for the pupils in your own school who regularly leave exams early. They will almost certainly be pupils who do not perform well in exams. It must be stressed again that if you have finished and checked your answers well before the end of the exam, then you are either not giving enough detail or paying attention to neatness and presentation.

Front Cover

The front cover of the exam paper asks you to fill in the information shown below.

Do this as neatly as possible and set off in the right direction. Remember this is the first thing that the marker will see when he sits down to mark your paper, so make a good impression.

Also on the front cover are some instructions about the exam. This is given for good reason and you should pay attention to what it says here. The instructions are the same for the General and the Credit exam.

Do not get confused by past exam papers before 2006 where the General exam required answers on spaces provided on the question paper but the Credit exam provided blank sheets of paper for the answers.

Since 2006 both the General and the Credit exam require the answers to be written on spaces provided on the question paper.

These are the instructions that you will see on the front of your exam paper.

Read each question carefully.
Answer **all** questions.
Write your answer on the space provided on the question paper.
Write as neatly as possible.
Answer in sentences wherever possible.

Before leaving the examination room you should give this book to the invigilator. If you do not, you may lose all the marks for this paper.

Grades

The Standard Grade computing studies exams assess the two components: Knowledge and Understanding (KU) and Problem Solving (PS).

The KU component is testing your ability to recall information about the content of the course material.

The PS component is testing your ability to apply your knowledge to a new situation, sometimes in a difficult and challenging way.

Both the KU and the PS are allocated roughly the same amounts of marks in the exam and you are given a grade for each component based, upon the table shown below.

Level	Percentage	Grade
Credit	70...100	1
Credit	50...69	2
General	70...100	3
General	50...69	4
Foundation	70...100	5
Foundation	50...69	6

The cut off scores for each grade can vary depending upon the level of difficulty of the exam, so do not feel that you must score at least 70% in the Credit exam to be awarded a grade of 1.

Each year, the examiner's report on the SQA website specifies the cut off scores for each grade in the Foundation, General and Credit exams.

Overall Grade Calculation

Your overall grade for Standard Grade computing studies is derived from your practical coursework grade as well as your performance in the exam.

The practical grade is derived from the coursework assessments that you have carried out in your own school and which are marked by your teacher. Your practical grade is an average of your performance in two programming tasks, two non programming tasks and a longer project that is chosen from a set list of projects published by the SQA.

Your overall grade for the course is derived from the formula:

Overall Grade = (KU Grade + PS Grade x 2 + Practical Grade x 2)/5

The examples given below show how the overall grade has been calculated for a cross section of pupils. (The overall grade is always rounded to the nearest whole number.)

Peter	**Grade**
Knowledge and Understanding	1
Problem solving	2
Practical Abilities	1
	(1 + 2 x **2** + 1 x **2**) / 5 = 7 / 5 = 1.4 =
	Overall Grade 1

Gillian	**Grade**
Knowledge and Understanding	2
Problem solving	4
Practical Abilities	3
	(2 + 4 x **2** + 3 x **2**) / 5 = 16 / 5 = 3.2 =
	Overall Grade 3

Martin	**Grade**
Knowledge and Understanding	3
Problem solving	6
Practical Abilities	4
	(3 + 6 x **2** + 4 x **2**) / 5 = 23 / 5 = 4.6 =
	Overall Grade <u>5</u>

Topic Index

	Exam A		Exam B		Exam C	
	General	Credit	General	Credit	General	Credit
General Purpose Packages						
Need						
Storage		3(b)				4(b)
Human Computer Interface	1(d), 7(d), (ii)		2(f)	1(b), (d)	1(e), (ii), 5(d)	1(d), 4(d), (ii)
Software Integration		1(c)	3(e)		5(c)	1(c)
Selection of Packages	7(b)	1(a)	2(e)	1(a), (ii)	2(a)	
Data Types						
Implications	1(e)	1(e)		2(h)	3(c)	7(d)
Advantages					2(b), (ii)	
Common Features	1(a)				2(b), (i)	1(e)
Word Processing	1(b), (c), (f)	1(f), (g), (h), 4(c)	2(a), (b), (c), (d)	4(a)	2(c), (d), (e), (f)	5(c)
Spreadsheet	6(a), (b), (c), (d), (e)	1(b), 2(a), (b), (c), (d), (e)	4(a), (b), (c), (d), (e), (f)	6(a), (b), (c), (d)	1(a), (b), (c), (d), (e), (i), (f)	1(a), (b), (f)
Database	5(a), (b), (c), (d)	4(b), (d)	5(a), (b), (c), (d)	2(b), (c), (d), (e), (g)	3(a), (b)	5(b)
Graphics	2(a), (b), (c), (d)		3(b), (c), (d)	3(c)	5(a), (e)	4(c)
Desk Top Publishing	2(e)			3(d)	4(a), (b)	4(d), (i)
Presentation and Multimedia		8(b), (c)		4(d)		6(a), (i)
Web Page Creation						5(d)
Expert Systems				7(c)	6(e)	5(e)
Communications and Networks						
Electronic Communication		3(a)	2(g)	1(c), (ii)	4(c)	
LANs and WANs		7(a), (b), (d)	6(a), (b), (c)			5(a), 5(g), (i)
Internet	7(c)	8(a), (d)	6(d)	1(c), (i), 7(d)	6(f), 8(d)	5(g), (ii)

	Exam A		Exam B		Exam C	
	General	Credit	General	Credit	General	Credit
Industrial Applications						
Need	4(e)				7(e)	2(a), (b)
Hardware and Software	4(a), (b), (c)	5(b), (c), (d)	8(a)	5(a), (b), (c), (d), 7(b)	7(d)	2(d), (i), (iii), (e), 7(a), (b)
Implications	4(d)	5(a)	8(b)		7(a), (b), (c)	2(c), 7(c)
Commercial Data Processing						
Need						3(c)
Data Processing Cycle	3(e), (f)					
Data Collection, Preparation and Input	3(a), (b), (g), 4(a)		1(b), (c), (ii)	2(f)	8(a)	3(a), (b)
Processing and Storage				7(a)	8(b)	
Output						
Hardware and Software			1(a)			
Implications	3(c), (d), 7(a)		1(c), (i), (f), 6(e)	8(a)	4(d), 8(c)	5(f)
Advantages						
Computer Systems						
Systems Software			7(b), (ii)			2(d), (ii)
Operating Systems	7(f), (g)	1(d)	7(c), (d)	1(e), 4(e)	6(d)	6(d)
Low Level Machine	8(a), (b), (c), (d)	3(c), (d), (i), 7(c)	3(a), 5(e), 7(b), (i)	2(a), 3(a), (b), 8(b), (ii), (c)	5(b)	3(d), (i), 4(a)
Hardware	7(d), (i), 7(e), 8(e)	3(a), 3(c), (d), (ii)	1(d), (e), 7(a)	1(a), (i), 4(b), (c), 8(b), (i), (d)	5(f), 6(a), (b), (c)	3(d), (ii), 6(a), (ii), (b), (c), (e)

Exam A – General Paper

Computing Studies Standard Grade: General

Practice Papers
For SQA Exams

General Level
Exam A

Fill in these boxes:

Name of centre	Town
Forename(s)	**Surname**

You are allowed 1 hour, 15 minutes to complete this paper.

Make sure you read the questions carefully.

Try to answer all of the questions in the time allowed.

Write your answers in the spaces provided.

Make sure you write as neatly as you can and answer in sentences wherever possible.

Leckie × Leckie
Scotland's leading educational publishers

KU PS

1. Sophie works as a journalist for a fashion magazine. She has written an article on ladies handbags for the next edition of the magazine.

(*a*) The editor asks Sophie to change the article so that paragraph 3 comes before paragraph 2.

Describe clearly the steps required to carry this out. PS 2

(*b*) One type of page layout used in word processing is portrait.

Name the other type of page layout. KU 1

(*c*) Sophie makes use of *standard paragraphs* in her work. Explain how the use of standard paragraphs can be used to improve Sophie's productivity. PS 1

(*d*) The word processing software has *on-line help* and an *on-line tutorial*.

Explain the difference between **on-line help** and an **on-line tutorial**. KU 2

(*e*) Sophie is worried about the security of her files.

State **two** ways in which Sophie can keep her files secure. KU 2

KU	PS

(*f*) All of the documents in the office are spell checked before a hardcopy is produced.

(i) The spellcheck highlights a client's name as an error even though it has been spelt correctly.

Why does this happen? **PS 1**

____

(ii) What can be done so that the spellcheck does not highlight this error in the future? **PS 1**

____

(iii) Sophie also uses a grammar check to find errors in her documents. Suggest two examples of errors that a grammar check would find. **PS 2**

____

____

____

____

2. (*a*) The circle and rectangle tool were used to create the graphic shown on the right:

Describe one **attribute** of the **circle tool** that has been altered. **PS 1**

____

(*b*) Name **one** tool that would be found in a painting program but not in a drawing program. **KU 1**

____

(*c*) What does it mean to **scale** a graphic? **KU 1**

____

____

	KU	PS

(*d*) State the editing that has been applied to the graphic below: **1** (PS)

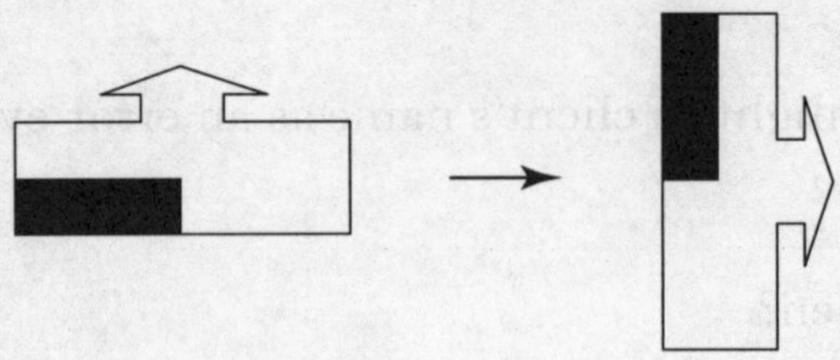

____

____

(*e*) Desk Top Publishing software combines two elements, one of which is graphics. What is the other element of DTP? **1** (KU)

____

____

3. Patients in a hospital put lines across boxes in the form below to order their breakfast.

Breakfast

Main Course		**Side Dish**		**Drink**	
Cereal	☐	Toast	☐	Tea	☐
Muesli	☐	Oatcakes	☐	Coffee	☐
Omelette	☐	Croissant	☐	Juice	☐
Porridge	☐			Milk	☐

Ward 1 ☐ 2 ☐ 3 ☐ **Bed No.** 1 ☐ 2 ☐ 3 ☐ 4 ☐ 5 ☐ 6 ☐ 7 ☐

(*a*) State the name that is given to a card like this that is used to enter data into a computer? **1** (KU)

____

____

(*b*) State **one** reason why this system is better than a using a keyboard to enter the data. **1** (PS)

____

____

____

KU | PS

(*c*) The hospital employed a *systems analyst* before the installation of the computerised system.

State **two** tasks that the systems analyst would have carried out. 2 (KU)

(*d*) State **one** running cost of the computer system. 1 (PS)

(*e*) State what the difference is between *data* and *information*? 1 (KU)

(*f*) (i) The hospital uses the Internet to buy goods and services for patient care.

State **one** advantage to the hospital of buying goods over the Internet. 1 (KU)

(ii) State **one** disadvantage of buying goods and services over the Internet. 1 (KU)

(*g*) The hospital pays for some of their goods by cheque. Banks use MICR to process cheques.

What do the initials MICR stand for? 1 (KU)

4. The robot arm shown to the right is to be used on a car assembly line.

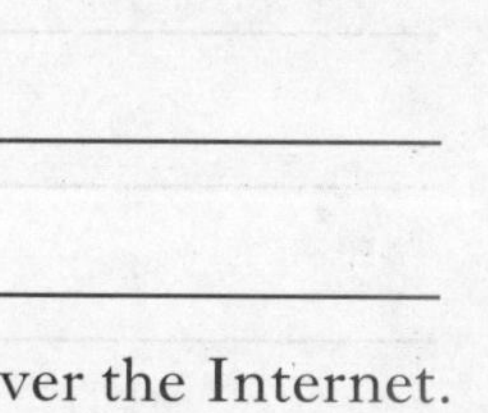

	KU	PS
(*a*) **State** which part of the robot arm allows it to perform yaw movements and **explain** the meaning of this term.	2	
(*b*) Describe **one** task that the robot arm could perform on the car production line and **name** an appropriate end effector for this task.		2
(*c*) Mobile robots operate in some warehouses storing and retrieving goods on the shelves. Describe **one** method that can be used to allow the mobile robots to find their way around the warehouse floor.	2	
(*d*) Some of the workers who worked on the production line before the robots had to be retrained to do other jobs. State a new job that would appear as a result of automation of the assembly plant.	1	
(*e*) State **one** advantage and **one** disadvantage of using robots instead of human labour.	2	

KU	PS

5. The secretary of a snooker club keeps a database file on the club members.

One of the records is shown below.

Name	David Wong
Address	12 White Street, Glasgow G12 9SU
Best Break	78
Sex	M
Date of Birth	19/11/87

(*a*) State a numeric field in the record above. 1

____

____

(*b*) The captain of the gent's team would like to be able to use the database to find out if a member would be willing to play in the team or not.

Explain how the record needs to be altered to allow him to do this. 2

____

____

____

____

KU	PS

(*c*) The secretary wants to find the player with the highest best break.

Explain how the secretary could use the database to quickly find the player with the highest best break. **2**

____

____

____

____

(*d*) The snooker club wishes to create a list of female members who were born after the 1st of April 1995. Choose **four** words from the list below to complete the paragraph to describe how the list can be produced.

sort	*is greater than*	*OR*
AND	*search*	*Sex*
is less than	*Name*	*equals*

Perform a complex ________ where the ________ field equals "Female"

________ the Date of Birth field ________ 01/04/95. **4**

6. A group of five pupils decided to use a spreadsheet to keep track of how many hours of television they watched during a week. The spreadsheet is shown below.

	A	B	C	D	E	F	G	H	I	J	K
1	TV										
2											
3		**Mon**	**Tue**	**Wed**	**Thu**	**Fri**	**Sat**	**Sun**	**Total**	**Highest**	
4	Andrew	2	1	2	3	4	8	5	25	8	
5	Stephani	3	3	2	5	0	0	8	21	8	
6	Helen	0	0	0	1	2	0	3	6	3	
7	Kirk	5	6	5	7	6	8	11	48	11	
8	Polly	1	1	1	0	2	4	7	16	7	

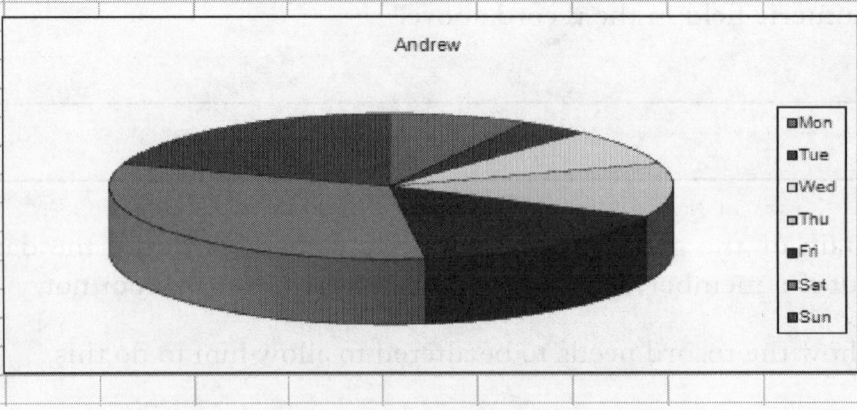

(*a*) Some of the values were automatically calculated using a formula.

In which cell would this formula appear?

(i) =B4+C4+D4+E4+F4+G4+H4 **1**

____

	KU	PS
(ii) The above formula could have been calculated using a function. Complete the function below: Sum = (______________________)	2	
(*b*) Cell J4 contains a function, part of which is shown below. Complete the function below: = __________ (________ : ________)		2
(*c*) The function entered into cell J4 is **replicated** down the column. State what is meant by the term *replication*. ____ ____	1	
(*d*) What can be done so that the full name of the pupil Stephanie can appear in column A? ____ ____ ____		1
(*e*) The graph shows Andrew's TV watching figures for the week. Explain clearly the steps required to produce this graph. ____ ____ ____ ____		2
7. Jasper Eagleburger writes articles for a music magazine in London. He lives in Oxford and each day spends 2 hours travelling to and from his work. A friend suggests to him that he could do most of his work at home and send it to his editor with the help of computer technology. (*a*) Which term is used to describe people who use computing technology to work from home? ____ ____	1	

	KU	PS
(*b*) State the general purpose package that would be best suited for Jasper use to create his articles. ____ ____	1	
(*c*) Jasper buys a laptop computer to write his articles for the magazine. Using some of the words and terms below, complete the sentences to describe how he can use the laptop computer to do his work. *broadband, dial-up, modem, search engine, hardware, browser* The computer that Jasper bought was Internet ready with ________ software already installed and it had a ________ to transmit data from the computer down the telephone line. Jasper opted for a ________ connection for its fast speed.		3
(*d*) (i) The laptop computer is connected to a printer. State whether an inkjet or a laser printer is best suited to Jasper's needs and **justify** your answer. ____ ____ ____ ____		2
(ii) Jasper used a wizard to help with the installation of the printer. State what is meant by a *wizard*? ____ ____	1	
(*e*) Sometimes Jasper wishes to include images on his articles. Name **one** input device that he could use to input images into his computer. ____ ____	1	

KU	PS

(*f*) When he finishes an article he saves the document on the hard disc of his computer. Tick (✓) **one** box which best describes the type of file that Jasper saves.

Program file ☐

Data file ☐

Database file ☐ — KU 1

(*g*) After a few months Jasper has hundreds of files saved on his hard disc and finds it hard to find previously saved files. What can he do to make it easier to find files on his hard disc? — PS 1

____

____

8. (*a*) (i) State how many *bits* there are in a *byte*. — KU 1

____

(ii) What is *machine code*? — KU 1

____

(*b*) A floppy disk with a storage capacity of 1.4 Megabytes contains the following two games programs:

Game Program	**Size**
4D Chess	424K
Karate Monkeys	916K

State how many Kilobytes of free space there are on the floppy disk. — PS 2

____

____

____

____

(*c*) Shown below is a diagram of a computer system.

Use the words below to complete the diagram.

Output, Processor, Hardcopy, Modem, Backing Store

Two have already been completed. — KU 3

KU	PS

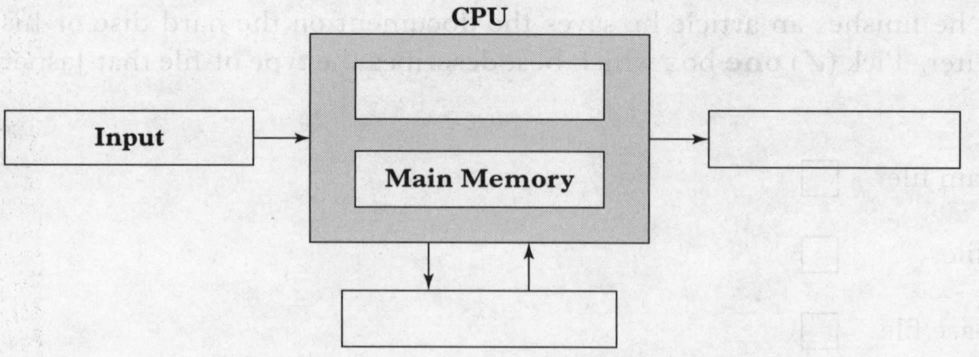

(*d*) State how text is stored on a computer system. **1**

____

____

(*e*) One part of main memory is called RAM.

State the other part. **1**

____

TOTAL MARKS **KU...36** **PS...36**

[End of Question Paper]

Exam A – Credit Paper

Computing Studies Standard Grade: Credit

Practice Papers
for SQA Exams

Credit Level
Exam A

Fill in these boxes:

Name of centre	Town

Forename(s)	Surname

You are allowed 1 hour, 45 minutes to complete this paper.

Make sure you read the questions carefully.

Try to answer all of the questions in the time allowed.

Write your answers in the spaces provided.

Make sure you write as neatly as you can and answer in sentences wherever possible.

Leckie × Leckie
Scotland's leading educational publishers

	KU	PS
1. Time of Your Life Books is a publishing company that publishes children's books. Mandy works as a secretary in the administration department. She uses a document in an integrated package to enter data on book sales and produce statistics and charts for the company managers.		

(*a*) State which application the integrated package is best suited to processing the data and creating charts. **[PS 1]**

____

____

____

(*b*) The charts that Mandy produces are fully labelled bar charts. State **two** suitable labels that can be added to a bar chart to make it fully labelled. **[KU 2]**

____

____

____

____

(*c*) The sales figures are updated at the end of each week. State whether a **static** link or a **dynamic** link should be used to link the data in the document with the chart and **justify** your answer. **[PS 2]**

____

____

____

____

	KU	PS

(*d*) Mandy wishes to print her documents and charts out on a new printer. The network manager tells her that he must install an item of software on her computer before she can do this.

State the item of software and describe its purpose. **KU 2**

____

____

____

____

(*e*) (i) The publishing company must conform to the requirements of the Data Protection Act. Describe two rights the data subject has with this Act. **KU 2**

____

____

____

____

(ii) The staff in Sophie's office has to conform to other Legal Acts concerned with computing.

State which Act is relevant to each of the following situations:

A Downloading music from the Internet.

B Sending a virus in an e-mail attachment. **KU 2**

____

____

____

(*f*) Mandy creates a report on sales figures at the end of each month as a word processing document which she e-mails to company managers in offices throughout Scotland. She uses the table feature in the layout.

Author	**Book**	**Sales**	**Cost/Book**

KU	PS

State **two** advantages of using the table feature in the layout. 2

____

____

____

____

(*g*) In a report an author's name has been mistakenly spelt as Mr Wiseman instead of Mr Weisman.

State which feature of word processing software could be used to correct this mistake in **one** operation. 1

____

____

(*h*) Mandy sometimes uses *templates* for word processing documents.

What is a template? 1

____

____

2. The company sells their books in four leading bookstores in Scotland. Below is part of a spreadsheet that shows the sales figures for the first four months of the year for one of their books entitled "School of Laughs".

	A	B	C	D	E	F	G	H
1	**Title**	**Price (£)**						
2	School of Laughs	12.9						
3								
4	**Shop**	**Jan**	**Feb**	**Mar**	**Apr**	**Total**	**Earnings**	**Sales**
5	Biggins Books	69	88	80	72	309	3986.1	OK
6	The Word Shop	134	156	158	182	630	8127	OK
7	Book Worm	49	30	56	48	183	2360.7	Poor
8	Books for Kids	213	245	254	198	910	11739	OK

(*a*) State a cell whose cell attributes should be changed to currency. 1

____

(*b*) State the formula that will be used in cell F5 to calculate the total number of copies of the book sold in the Biggins Books shop. 1

____

KU	PS

(*c*) The formula in cell F5 is to be replicated into cells F6 to F8.

Which type of cell referencing is required? Explain your answer. **2** (KU)

____

____

____

(*d*) The formula in cell G5 calculates the earnings for the sales in Biggins Books for the first four months of the year. This formula is replicated into cells G6 to G8.

(i) State the formula that is required to be entered into cell G5. **2** (PS)

____

____

____

(ii) Explain why the formula in G5 requires an absolute cell reference. **1** (PS)

____

____

____

(*e*) If fewer than 200 copies of a book are sold then the company managers visit the shop to try and improve the sales of the book.

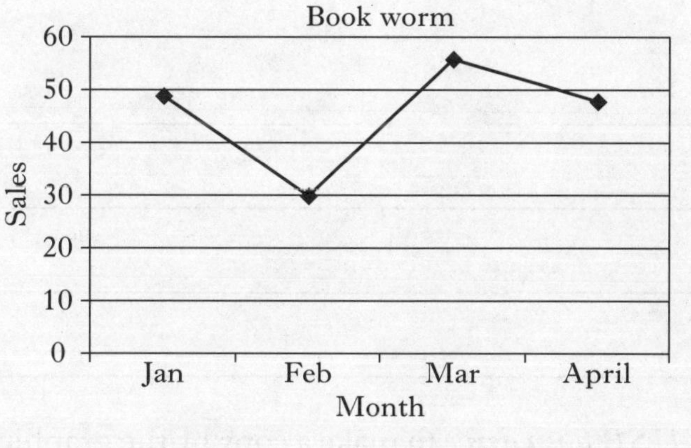

Complete the function in H5 which is shown below to display the text "Poor" if sales are fewer than 200 and "OK" if they are 200 or more.

= _________ (__________, "Poor", __________) **3** (PS)

KU	PS

3. The company has an art works department which designs a black and white logo to appear on the front of their books. The initial design is drawn on paper.

Leckie×Leckie
Scotland's leading educational publishers

1280 pixels

2400 pixels

(*a*) The company has offices in cities throughout Scotland.

Explain how computing technology can be used to send the paper design quickly to company offices in different cities. 2

___

___

___

(*b*) (i) The graphic file is saved in a standard file format.

State one advantage in saving the file in a standard file format. 1

___

___

(ii) State a standard file format for graphics. 1

___

(*c*) Calculate the storage requirements of this graphic in kilobytes. Show all your working. 3

___

___

___

___

(*d*) An employee uses a *USB flash drive* to make a copy of the graphic file to show to a friend who is an artist. The flash drive has 2Mb of free storage space.

(i) State if there is enough free space on the flash drive to store the image and show a calculation to support your answer. 2

___

___

___

KU	PS

(ii) State **one** reason why a USB flash drive is more suitable to store the file than a CD. **1** (KU)

____

4. Time of Your Life Books keeps details on their authors in a database. The database currently holds information concerning 280 authors. One of the records in the database is shown below.

Field Name	**Sample Data**
Sex	F
Firstname	Sophie
Surname	Davidson
Date of Birth	120678
Address	63 Hammond Road
Town	Edinburgh
Postcode	EH1 7QY

(*a*) Explain how the data entered into the **Sex** field can be validated. **2** (PS)

____

____

____

(*b*) The company wants to produce a paper copy of all the female authors who live in Glasgow.

Describe how this could be done. **3** (PS)

____

____

____

____

	KU	PS
(*c*) Each year a personalised letter is sent to all the authors inviting them to a Christmas party using mail merge. Outline the steps involved in producing these letters.	3	

	KU	PS
(*d*) (i) State what a computed field is.	1	
(ii) State how a computed field can save time when entering data.		2

5. Time of Your Life Books have a warehouse where they store their publications before distribution to the shops. Stationary robots have recently been installed in the warehouse to automate the process of packing the books into boxes and mobile robots to take them to pick up points for loading onto vans.

(*a*) Some of the company managers were worried that the introduction of the robots would lead to a very high electricity bill.

State **one** reason why the electricity bill might increase and **one** reason why it might decrease as a result of the introduction of the robots. — PS 2

KU	PS

(*b*) The system used to pack the books into boxes uses intelligent robots.

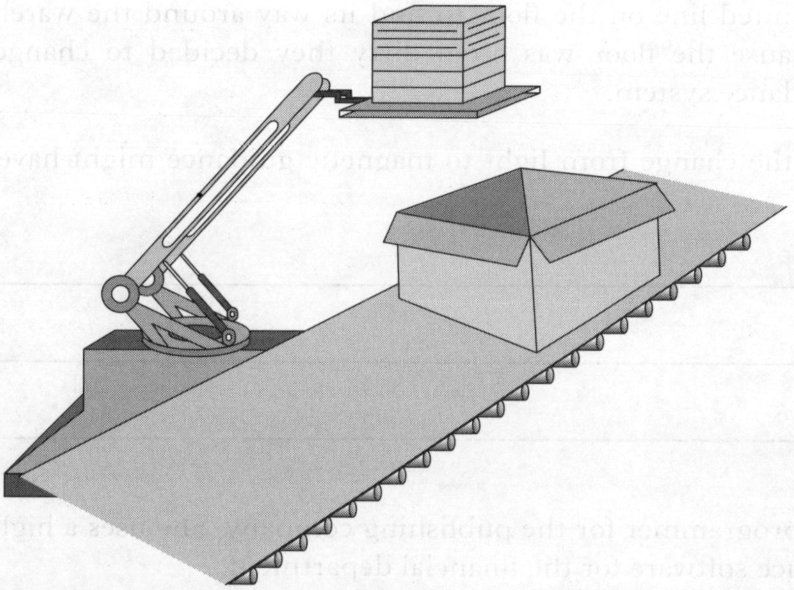

(i) State what is meant by an intelligent robot. **1** (KU)

(ii) State a hardware device that an intelligent robot requires in order to demonstrate intelligent behavior. **1** (PS)

(*c*) The robots have a program stored in a ROM chip which was written in a control language.

(i) State **two** advantages of storing the program in a ROM chip. **2** (KU)

	KU	PS
(ii) State why the program is written in a control language.		1
(*d*) Initially the mobile robots used a light guidance system where the robot followed a painted line on the floor to find its way around the warehouse. However because the floor was often dirty they decided to change to a magnetic guidance system. Explain why the change from light to magnetic guidance might have been necessary.		1

6. Rosie works as a programmer for the publishing company. She uses a high level language to produce software for the financial department.

(*a*) State **two** common features of high level languages. **2** (KU)

	KU	PS
(*b*) If someone was learning to program in a high level language, which type of translator would you recommend they use? Explain your answer.		2
(*c*) Rosie would like her program to be *portable*. Explain the term **portable**.	1	
(*d*) The operating system on Rosie's computer has *foreground/background* job capability which Rosie uses when she needs to print out her programs. Describe what is meant by **background** printing and how it can be a help to Rosie.	2	
7. A company has 20 desktop computers that are connected up in a LAN with a file server and a print server.		
(*a*) What item of hardware do the computers require in order to be connected to a LAN?	1	
(*b*) State the function of the file server on this network.	1	
(*c*) The desktop computers have a processor which contains a control unit. State **one** other component on a processor and describe its purpose.	2	

	KU	PS

(*d*) The computers are currently connected using cables but there are plans to move to wireless technology.

(i) State an **advantage** of using wireless technology. — PS 1

(ii) State a **disadvantage** of using wireless technology. — PS 1

8. Time of Your Life Books has a website where they advertise and sell their books.

(*a*) State a language that is used to create websites. — KU 1

(*b*) When the website was being developed, the creators had to capture images of authors and book covers for the site.

State **two** ways of capturing these images for the website. — KU 2

(*c*) The developers wanted to make the website attractive to people visiting their site by using a lot of multimedia content.

Apart from text and images, give an example of how other multimedia elements could be used to advertise the books. — PS 1

KU	PS

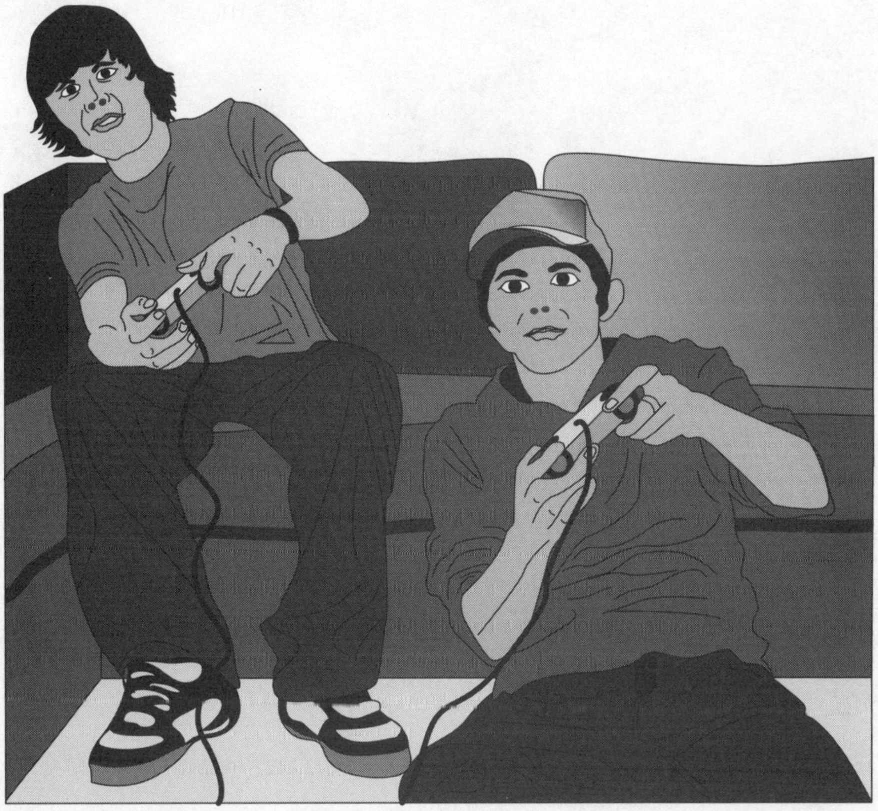

(*d*) The website includes games software to attract children to the site. The software can be downloaded for a trial period after which it must be paid for or deleted. State the name of this type of software. 1

____

____

TOTAL MARKS **KU...36** **PS...36**

[End of Question Paper]

Exam B – General Paper

Computing Studies Standard Grade: General

Practice Papers
For SQA Exams

General Level
Exam B

Fill in these boxes:

Name of centre	Town
Forename(s)	**Surname**

You are allowed 1 hour, 15 minutes to complete this paper.

Make sure you read the questions carefully.

Try to answer all of the questions in the time allowed.

Write your answers in the spaces provided.

Make sure you write as neatly as you can and answer in sentences wherever possible.

Leckie × Leckie
Scotland's leading educational publishers

KU	PS

1. Louise is a customer of a national bank. The bank has a **mainframe** computer which is used to store and process data.

(*a*) Give **two** reasons why the bank uses a mainframe computer to process data. — PS: 2

____

____

____

____

(*b*) The bank uses MICR to process their cheques. Give one advantage of using MICR. — KU: 1

____

____

(*c*) (i) Louise has a credit card which she uses in supermarkets to pay for her shopping by EFT.

What do the initials EFT stand for?

E____________ F____________ T____________ — KU: 1

KU	PS

(ii) If the barcode on an article is not scanned properly at the checkout then the computer makes a beep to indicate that an error has taken place.

What is added to a barcode to allow scanning errors to be detected? **1** (KU)

____

(*d*) (i) The bank cashline system has to store the account details of millions of customers.

Tick (✓) **one** box which gives the most suitable backing store for the cashline system.

Floppy disc ☐

Hard disc ☐

Magnetic tape ☐ **1** (KU)

(ii) The cashline system for the bank uses a *touch sensitive screen.*

State an advantage to the customers of using a touch sensitive screen instead of a keypad to enter data? **1** (PS)

____

____

(*e*) The bank's branches all have laser printers because of their high speed of printing. Which term is used to describe the speed of a printer? **1** (KU)

____

(*f*) Some of the bank's customers use *on-line banking* to manage their accounts.

(i) Suggest **one** way in which the customers can make use of on-line banking. **1** (PS)

____

____

(ii) State a concern that a bank customer might have in using on-line banking. **1** (PS)

____

____

	KU	PS

2. A sports club uses a word processing program to produce posters and booking sheets for activities. The squash booking sheet is shown below.

MON JUNE 12TH					
Court 1		**Court 2**		**Court 3**	
Time	**Name**	**Time**	**Name**	**Time**	**Name**
12:00 – 13:00		12:00 – 13:00		12:00 – 13:00	
13:00 – 14:00		13:00 – 14:00		13:00 – 14:00	
14:00 – 15:00		14:00 – 15:00		14:00 – 15:00	
15:00 – 16:00		15:00 – 16:00		15:00 – 16:00	
16:00 – 17:00		16:00 – 17:00		16:00 – 17:00	
17:00 – 18:00		17:00 – 18:00		17:00 – 18:00	
18:00 – 19:00		18:00 – 19:00		18:00 – 19:00	
19:00 – 20:00		19:00 – 20:00		19:00 – 20:00	
20:00 – 21:00		20:00 – 21:00		20:00 – 21:00	

(*a*) Which page layout has been used for this document? **1** (KU)

(*b*) Describe **one** advantage of using a table in this document. **1** (PS)

(*c*) State the alignment which has been used in the cell containing the text "Court 1". **1** (KU)

(*d*) The sports club manager has decided to allow members to book the squash courts between 11:00–12:00. State how the table can be edited to allow members to book courts at this time. **1** (PS)

(*e*) The sports club uses a general purpose package to store member details.

(i) Which general purpose package is best suited to this situation? **1** (PS)

(ii) State **two** reasons for your answer. **2** (PS)

	KU	PS

(*f*) The computers in the sports club make use of a WIMP Human Computer Interface.

(i) What do the initials WIMP stand for?

W__________ I__________ M__________ P__________ **1**

(ii) What effect does a WIMP HCI have on the user friendliness of a computer? **1**

____

____

(*g*) One of the secretaries regularly sends e-mails to members which are written in CAPITAL LETTERS. Which rule of *netiquette* is the secretary breaking? **1**

____

____

3. A musical instrument company sells pianos and guitars.

The company logo was created in a graphics program.

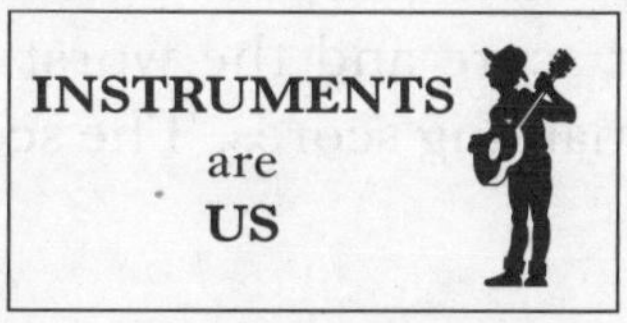

(*a*) Explain how a black and white graphic is stored on a computer. **1**

____

(*b*) The logo above is to be edited to look like the logo shown below.

State how the company created this logo from the original logo. **3** (PS)

____

____

____

____

	KU	PS

(*c*) What does it mean to rotate a graphic? **KU 1**

____

____

(*d*) The graphics program used to create the logo has a line tool.

State **two** attributes of a line tool. **KU 2**

____

____

____

(*e*) Why might the musical company have chosen an individual graphics program rather than a graphics program that is part of an integrated package? **PS 1**

____

____

4. An ice skating competition uses a general purpose package to enter and process the scores from 6 judges. The best score and the worst score are not counted. The total score is the sum of the remaining scores. The scores for one competitor are shown below.

	A	B	C	D	E	F	G	H
1	**Competitor**	**Judge1**	**Judge2**	**Judge3**	**Judge4**	**Judge5**	**Judge6**	
2	Henrik Fashbecker	5.6	5.3	5.7	4.9	5	5.8	
3								
4	**Best Score**	5.8						
5	**Worst Score**	4.9						
6	**Total Score**	21.6						
7								

(*a*) Which type of general purpose package was used to create this document? **KU 1**

____

(*b*) In which cell would this formula appear?

=MIN(B2:G2) **PS 1**

____

(*c*) Write down the formula that has been entered into cell B6. **PS 2**

____

____

KU PS

(*d*) State **two** ways in which the cell formatting applied to cell A1 differs from that applied to cell B1. 2

(*e*) Explain what can be done to the number in cell F2 so that it is displayed as 5.0 instead of 5. 1

(*f*) Some of the cells have been locked so that their contents cannot be changed.

What name is given to the feature that allows this to be done? 1

5. A shoe shop keeps a database file of their stock of shoes.

One of the records is shown below.

Type of Shoe	High heel
Size	6
Sex	Female
Age Group	Adult
Price (£)	39.95

(*a*) State **two** field types used in this database. 2

(*b*) The sales staff in the shop need to know if a particular shoe is in stock.

State how the database can be amended to allow this to happen. 2

	KU	PS

(*c*) The manager of the shop would like to find out which are the highest priced shoes.

Explain how the database could be used to find the highest priced shoes. **2**

____

____

____

____

(*d*) A customer wishes to know what size 6 children's shoes the shop has in stock.

Choose **three** words from the list below to complete the paragraph which describes how these shoes can be selected from the database.

sort	*Child*	*is greater than*
OR	*Price (£)*	*search*
is less than	*equals*	*Type of Shoe*

Perform a complex ______________ where the Age Group field equals ______________ AND the Size field ______________ 6. **3**

(*e*) Each record requires 120 bytes of storage space.

If the database has 640 records, how many Kilobytes are required to store the complete database file? **2**

____

____

____

	KU	PS

6. A small flower shop in Dumfries has 4 stand-alone computers which it uses to manage the business.

(*a*) (i) The owner of the flower shop decides to connect the computers in the shop together in a LAN.

What do the initials LAN stand for?

L______________ Area N______________ **1**

(ii) State the name given to the type of network which connects computers together over a large geographical area. **1**

____

(*b*) One reason for installing a computer network was to share peripherals.

State a peripheral device that could be shared on this network. **1**

____

(*c*) State **three** ways of improving the security of a computer network. **3**

____

____

____

____

____

KU	PS

(*d*) The flower shop has its own website to advertise its flowers.

(i) State the language used to create web pages. 1

____

(ii) State how new customers could find the shop's website on the Internet. 2

____

____

____

(*e*) Sometimes the shop has to call out a computer *engineer* to help with their computer system. State **one** task that would be carried out by a computer engineer. 1

____

____

7. Different types of computers have different input, output and storage devices.

(*a*) Select **six** words from the list below to complete the paragraph which describes different types of computer.

stylus	*touch sensitive*	*robust*
TFT	*laptop*	*digital camera*
portable	*scanner*	*palmtop*

A ______________ and a desktop computer have QWERTY keyboards to enter data whereas a ______________ computer uses a ______________ to write on a ______________________ screen. A desktop computer is less ______________ than the other two types of computer but usually has a large ______________________ screen display. 6

(*b*) (i) What is the name of the programming language where the instructions are written in binary codes? 1

____

____

KU	PS

(ii) Describe **two** features of a high level programming language. 2

____

____

____

(*c*) Computers have an operating system.

Tick (✓) **one** box which gives the most suitable description of an operating system.

A general purpose package. ☐

A device used to control the computer. ☐

A computer program. ☐ 1

(*d*) What is a directory on a disk? 1

____

8. A virtual reality simulator is used to train pilots for the Royal Air Force.

(*a*) (i) The virtual reality system is an example of a *real time system.*

Explain the term real time system. 1

____

(ii) Why is a real time system essential for the simulator? 1

____

	KU	PS
(*b*) Despite a high initial expenditure there are long term savings of using the simulator.		
Describe **two** ways in which the simulator can save money in the long term.		2

Total Marks **KU…36** **PS…36**

[End of Question Paper]

Exam B – Credit Paper

Computing Studies   Standard Grade: Credit

Practice Papers
For SQA Exams

Credit Level
Exam B

Fill in these boxes:

Name of centre	Town

Forename(s)	Surname

You are allowed 1 hour, 45 minutes to complete this paper.

Make sure you read the questions carefully.

Try to answer all of the questions in the time allowed.

Write your answers in the spaces provided.

Make sure you write as neatly as you can and answer in sentences wherever possible.

Leckie × Leckie
Scotland's leading educational publishers

KU	PS

1. Fiona works as a secretary in the tourist office in a small town in the Scottish Highlands. She uses an integrated package to do administration work for the office.

(*a*) One of her tasks is to store information on local hotels on computer so that the details can be given to people over the telephone.

(i) State which backing store device is suitable for this situation and **justify** your answer. — PS: 2

____

____

____

____

(ii) Peter often has to search quickly for hotels which meet the requirements of the people looking for accommodation.

Explain why a database is the most suitable general purpose package to store the hotel details? — KU: 2

____

____

____

____

(*b*) Fiona has poor eyesight and sometimes finds it hard to make out what is on her computer screen.

State **one** way in which the Human Computer Interface could be customised on her computer to make it easier for Fiona to do her work. — PS: 1

____

____

(*c*) All of the computers in the tourist office have an Internet connection which is used to send and reply to e-mails and download multimedia files about local attractions.

(i) State **two** reasons why the employees in the tourist office would find a broadband connection is better than a dial-up connection. — KU: 2

____

____

____

____

	KU	PS

(ii) When replying to inquiries Fiona takes care to conform to the rules of *netiquette*. Explain the term netiquette. **1** (KU)

(*d*) Lots of templates are used for word processing and spreadsheet documents.

State how templates can improve the productivity of the office employees. **1** (PS)

(*e*) Last week a laser printer was bought for Fiona's computer and at the same time a printer driver was installed on the computer.

Describe a printer driver. **1** (KU)

2. Culdoran High School uses a database to store their students' details.

Part of the database design is shown below.

Field Name	Size (Bytes)	Sample Record
Student Code	5	DMOR7
Firstname	20	David
Surname	20	Morrison
Address	30	7 North Street
Town	20	Glasgow
Postcode	7	G12 6YB
Telephone No.	11	0141 667345
Sex	1	M
Date of Birth	6	031198

(*a*) The School's database file currently holds information concerning 680 students.

Calculate the storage capacity of the database file in kilobytes. **2** (PS)

	KU	PS
(*b*) State a suitable **data type** for each of these fields: (i) Town (ii) Date of Birth.	2	
(*c*) Describe how the database could be used to produce a list of male students who live in Edinburgh.		2
(*d*) The Student Code field is calculated automatically using other fields in the database. State the name given to this type of field.	1	
(*e*) When the telephone numbers were entered into the database, it was necessary to scroll through all the other fields in each record. State how the input format can be changed to make it easier to enter the telephone numbers.		2
(*f*) When entering data into the database validation and verification are used to make sure that the data is correct. Describe how verification and validation helps to detect and remove errors.	2	

KU	PS

(*g*) There are 6 students in the school who live in Stirling whose records have been selected for a report. The report has been generated with the layout shown below.

Firstname	Surname	Sex	Telephone No.
Samantha	Black	F	01786 334236
Alice	Forsythe	F	01786 990301
Mandy	Morris	F	01786 022031
Helen	Watkins	F	01786 998920
Tom	Davidson	M	01786 465582
Martin	Paterson	M	01786 777278

Explain how the report has been achieved by mentioning changes to the output format and the sorting that has taken place. **2**

(*h*) The school is concerned that some of the sixth year students are attempting to hack into the computer system and tamper with the data in the database. They are also worried that they are open to a virus attack.

State the law that makes hacking and sending viruses illegal. **1**

3. A book on how to make cut out silhouettes contains two graphics of a silhouette on each of 120 pages. Each silhouette is a black and white graphic.

An example of one of the silhouettes is shown below.

500 pixels

240 pixels

(*a*) Calculate the storage requirement for the black and white graphic shown above which has 500 × 240 pixels. (Give your answer in bytes or appropriate units.) **Show all of your working.** **2**

	KU	PS

(b) Calculate the storage requirements of all the silhouettes in the book. (Give your answer in Megabytes.) **2** (PS)

(c) State the graphics tool that has been used to edit the image as shown below. **1** (KU)

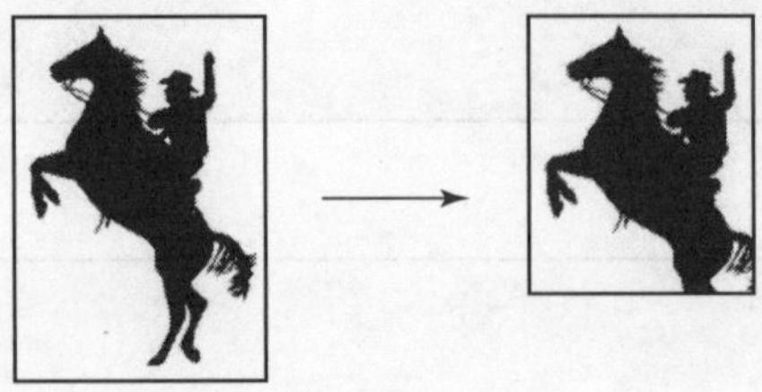

(d) (i) The book was created using a desktop publishing package.

State why desktop publishing software is appropriate to this task. **1** (PS)

(ii) When the book was being created it was found that some of the images were being covered over with text. Explain how this problem can be put right. **1** (PS)

4. Alice is a lecturer in the College of Fine Arts. She has hundreds of pages of lecture notes that she has produced over the years for the courses that she teaches.

Recently a computer virus destroyed all the data files in the college and the only copy Alice has of her lecture notes is on paper.

(a) Explain how Alice can enter her lecture notes into a computer without typing them all in again. **1** (PS)

KU	PS

(*b*) The computer that Alice uses has a *TFT* screen.

What do the initials TFT stand for? **1** (KU)

____

(*c*) Sometimes, she wishes to make copies of her files so that she can work on them at home. One of her files has a capacity of 12.3 Mb.

State a suitable backing storage device that Alice could use to make a copy of this file and **justify** your answer. **2** (PS)

____

____

____

(*d*) Alice is applying for a job as department head and has been invited to an interview where she has to give a presentation using a multimedia presentation package.

(i) Describe **two** differences between a multimedia presentation package and a multimedia authoring package. **2** (KU)

____

____

____

(ii) Her presentation uses a *linear linkage of slides* but she would like to be able to go back to previous slides when giving the slide show if necessary.

Describe a way in which she could do this. **1** (PS)

____

____

____

(*e*) Alice organises the files that she saves into folders as shown below.

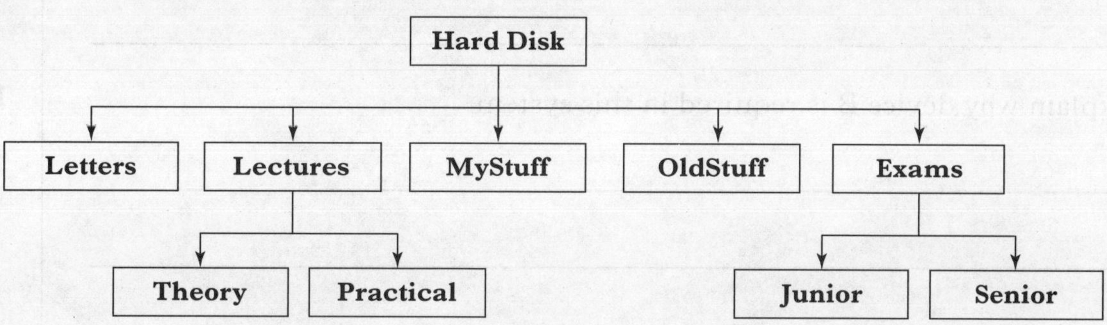

KU	PS

(i) State the name given to this type of filing system. 1

(ii) State **two** advantages of using this filing system. 2

5. A chemical reaction to produce gloss paint is controlled by a computer system.

Data on the pressure of the reaction container is entered into a computer.

The computer outputs a signal to adjust the pressure by opening and closing a valve in the reaction chamber.

The diagram below represents the computer system.

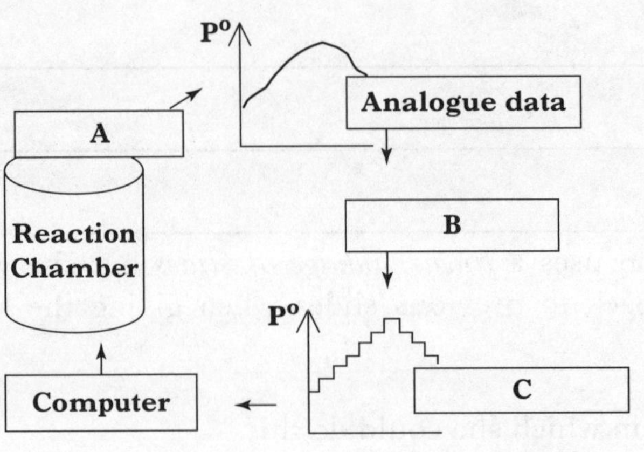

(*a*) Identify the labels A, B and C. 3

(*b*) Explain why device B is required in this system. 1

KU	PS

(*c*) The program to control this system is stored in a ROM chip.

State **one** reason for using a ROM chip. 1

(*d*) State what is meant by an *embedded system*. 1

6. A school cook uses a spreadsheet to store the weekly tuck shop sales.

Part of the spreadsheet is shown below:

	A	B	C	D	E	F	G
1		**Price**			**Doughnut**	**Meringue**	**Takings**
2	**Doughnut**	0.4		Mon	10	5	5.5
3	**Meringue**	0.3		Tue	14	3	6.5
4				Wed	10	6	5.8
5				Thu	8	4	4.4
6				Fri	19	7	9.7
7						**Total**	**31.9**
8	**Target**	No					

(*a*) The cell attributes of cells G2 to G6 are to be altered.

(i) State what is meant by the term 'cell attribute'. 1

(ii) State a suitable alteration to the cell attributes of these cells. 1

(*b*) Cell G2 contains a formula to calculate the total takings for Monday.

This formula is then replicated for the other days.

(i) Explain the term replicated. 1

(ii) Write down the formula that has been entered into cell G2. 2

	KU	PS

(c) The tuck shop is to be opened on Sat for the students who come to sports clubs.

The cook decides to add the Saturday sales to the spreadsheet.

State how the data for Saturday can be added to the spreadsheet. PS 1

____

(d) The cook tries to reach target takings of £50 each week.

Cell B8 contains a function that automatically displays the text "Yes" or "No" depending on whether the target has been reached or not

Part of the function is shown below.

Copy and complete the function.

= __________ (__________, "Yes",__________) PS 3

7. Wendy works as a trainee vet in a private practice.

(a) The practice holds data on the animals and their treatment on a database.

Sometimes, the database has to be able to be accessed by secretaries and vets at the same time.

State the name given to this type of database. KU 1

____

(b) Wendy has been on a course where she was taught how to perform surgery on animals using a virtual reality system.

(i) State what is meant by the term virtual reality. KU 1

____

(ii) State **two** advantages of using virtual reality to train vets to perform surgery. KU 2

____

____

____

____

KU	PS

(*c*) In the waiting room there is a computer running an expert system. This program allows owners to enter information about themselves which it uses to give advice on which breed of dog is best suited to them as a pet.

(i) State an example of a rule or fact that could be stored in this expert system. **PS 1**

____

____

(ii) State an advantage of using an expert system in this situation. **PS 1**

____

____

(*d*) Sometimes the vets make home visits to elderly pet owners who find it hard to travel into the practice. The vets use mobile Internet technology to access vet websites during their visits.

(i) Describe **two** mobile Internet technologies. **KU 2**

____

____

____

____

(ii) State what the term ISP stands for. **KU 1**

____

____

	KU	PS
8. Banks that use the Internet to do business are concerned about computing fraud.		
(*a*) State **two** measures that banks can take to improve the security of their transactions.	2	
(*b*) Main memory is made up of RAM and ROM.		
(i) When a user loads up a program from the hard disk into main memory, is it loaded into RAM or ROM?		1
(ii) Describe how individual storage locations in main memory are identified by a processor.	1	
(*c*) State the name given to a group of bits that is transferred within the CPU as a single unit.	1	
(*d*) State the function of a graphics card in a computer system.	1	

Total Marks **KU…36** **PS…36**

[End of Question Paper]

Exam C – General Paper

Computing Studies Standard Grade: General

Practice Papers
For SQA Exams

General Level
Exam C

Fill in these boxes:

Name of centre	Town

Forename(s)	Surname

You are allowed 1 hour, 15 minutes to complete this paper.

Make sure you read the questions carefully.

Try to answer all of the questions in the time allowed.

Write your answers in the spaces provided.

Make sure you write as neatly as you can and answer in sentences wherever possible.

Leckie × Leckie
Scotland's leading educational publishers

KU	PS

1. A newsagents makes uses of a spreadsheet to show the wages of their paper boys.

	A	B	C	D	E	F
1	Paper Boy	Time of Day	Basic Pay	Number of Papers	Total Pay	
2	Harry	Morning	18	27	20.7	
3	Fred	Morning	18	19	19.9	
4	Tom	Evening	15	16	16.6	
5	Jamie	Morning	18	34	21.4	
6	Dick	Morning	18	23	20.3	
7	Alan	Evening	15	19	16.9	
8	Walter	Evening	15	17	16.7	
9						

The Total Pay is calculated from a Basic Pay plus an extra £0.10 per paper delivered. Paper boys who do a morning run get £18 Basic Pay and those who do the evening run get £15.

(*a*) Write down the formula that has been entered into cell E2. **2** (PS)

___

___

(*b*) Once the formula had been entered into cell E2 to calculate the Total Pay for Harry, a similar formula was required for the other paper boys.

State the feature of the spreadsheet that could be used to produce the formula in cells E3 to E8. **1** (KU)

___

___

(*c*) State what needs to be done to the numbers in columns C, D and E so that they are displayed in pounds and pence. **1** (KU)

___

___

(*d*) Jamie gives up his paper round to spend more time on his homework. State how the spreadsheet can be amended to remove Jamie. **1** (PS)

___

___

	KU	PS

(*e*) (i) Describe how the spreadsheet can be used to produce the bar chart shown below. **2** (PS)

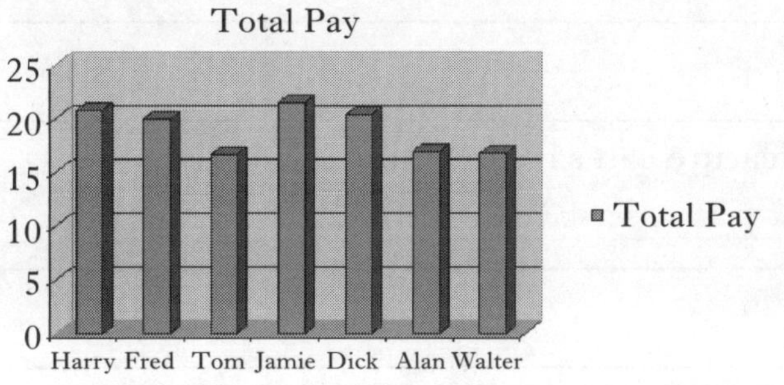

____

____

____

____

(ii) The bar chart was created by using a feature of the software that guided the user through the task in a series of steps.
What name is given to this type of feature? **1** (KU)

____

(*f*) A function to calculate the average total pay is to be entered into cell E9.

Write down this function. **2** (PS)

____

____

2. Alice is a best selling author who writes her books at home.

(*a*) Alice uses a general purpose package to write her books.

Tick (✓) **one** box which gives the general purpose packages most suitable for writing a book.

Word processing ☐

Database ☐

Graphics ☐ **1** (KU)

	KU	PS
(*b*) (i) State the feature that Alice can use to automatically put page numbers on the bottom of each page.	1	
(ii) State how this feature can save her time.		1
(*c*) In her latest book Alice has typed the heroine's name "Sophie" several times, but would like to change it to "Stephanie". Describe an efficient way of changing the heroine's name.		2
(*d*) Alice notices that the word processing program uses ***word-wrap***. Explain the term word-wrap.	1	
(*e*) At the end of the first chapter of her book, she finishes half way down a page and would like to start the next chapter at the top of the next page. State a feature of word processing that would allow her to do this.	1	
(*f*) Her publisher insists that there should be no more than 600 words on a page but, on checking, she notices that some pages have more than this. (i) How can Alice quickly check how many words there are on a page?		2
(ii) State **two** ways in which she can reduce the number of words on a page without deleting any text.		2

KU	PS

3. Lauren South is the owner of a beauty clinic. She keeps details on her 200 clients on a computer database.

Ten records are shown below.

Surname	**First Name**	**Age**	**Last Visit**	**Treatment**
Walters	Mandy	55	12/05/09	Facial
Davidson	Gwen	42	07/02/07	Facial
Robbins	Betty	35	31/03/09	Facial
Swanson	Sophie	21	19/04/09	Facial
Macdonald	Polly	58	24/12/08	Liposuction
Green	Ann	43	06/12/09	Liposuction
Lamont	Helen	39	16/02/09	Liposuction
Paterson	Florence	49	28/01/08	Waxing
Hampshire	Wendy	44	09/04/09	Waxing
Macgregor	Helen	18	30/05/09	Waxing

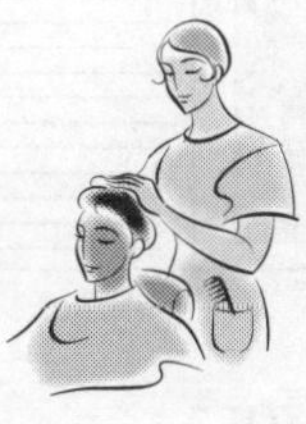

(*a*) (i) State the number of fields in this database. **1**

____

(ii) State which field type is the **Last Visit** field. **1**

____

(iii) State another field that could be included in this database and give the field type of this field. **2**

____

____

(*b*) The database above has been sorted on two fields.

Complete the sentence using the words below.

Age	*Treatment*	*record*
ascending	*descending*	*First Name*
	Surname	

A complex sort has been performed with the ______________ field

in ____________________ order and the ____________________ field

in ______________ order. **4**

(*c*) State how the beauty clinic can protect itself against accidental or deliberate loss of the database file.

____

KU	PS
	1

4. The Daily Trumpet newspaper uses DTP software to produce their paper.

(*a*) (i) What do the initials DTP stand for?

D____________ Top P____________

KU	PS
1	

(ii) Which of the following is NOT an element of DTP?

Tick (✓) **one** box which gives an element which is NOT part of DTP.

Graphics ☐

Video ☐

Text ☐

KU	PS
1	

(*b*) Sometimes the front page of the newspaper is created from a *template*.

State what is meant by a template.

____

____

KU	PS
1	

(*c*) The reporters send their articles into the newspaper office by *e-mail*.

(i) State **two** advantages of the reporters sending in e-mails instead of hardcopies of their articles by post.

____

____

KU	PS
	2

KU	PS

(ii) State **one** disadvantage of sending e-mails. 1 (KU)

(*d*) The newspaper office employs a *network manager* and a *programmer* to help with their computer system.

(i) State **two** tasks carried out by a network manager. 2 (KU)

(ii) State **two** tasks carried out by a programmer. 2 (KU)

5. An Edinburgh hockey club used a graphics program to design a logo for their team tracksuits. They used the circle and text tool to produce the two possible designs shown below.

(a) State two ways in which the second logo is different from the first logo. 2 (PS)

(*b*) How are graphics represented on a computer system. 1 (KU)

Tick (✓) **one** box which best describes how graphics are stored on a computer.

ASCII codes. ☐

Binary numbers ☐

Binary codes for colours of pixels ☐

(*c*) (i) The graphics program is part of an *integrated package*.

State what is meant by an integrated package.

KU	PS

1

(ii) State why it is easier to learn how to use a graphics program that is part of an integrated package than an individual graphics program. 1

(*d*) The software used to produce the newspaper has several *toolbars*.

State what is meant by the term toolbar. 1

(*e*) Graphics packages have editing tools to manipulate the images.

Tick (✓) **one** box which indicates a graphics editing tool. 1

Searching ☐

Scaling ☐

Mail merge ☐

(*f*) The graphics file was printed out on a *laser printer* which the club had recently bought to replace an *inkjet printer*.

(i) State **one** advantage of a laser printer over an inkjet printer. 1

(ii) State the term used to indicate the resolution of a printer. 1

6. A computer shop sells computer *hardware* and *software*. The shop specialises in *backing store devices*.

(*a*) State a **portable** backing store device that could be used to transfer data between computers. 1

(*b*) (i) State **one** input device that the shop might sell. 1

(ii) State **one** output device that the shop might sell. 1

KU | PS

(*c*) The shop provides the service of upgrading computers for their customers.

A lot of customers ask for an increase in the amount of *RAM* on their computers.

(i) What do the initials RAM stand for? — KU 1

R________________ Access M________________

(ii) State one advantage of increasing the amount of RAM on a computer. — PS 1

(ii) RAM is one component of main memory. State the other component of main memory. — KU 1

(*d*) State the name of the program which manages the hardware of a computer system. — KU 1

(*e*) The shop has an item of *software* to assist them in diagnosing faults and repair of computers.

State the name given to this type of software. — KU 1

(*f*) The address of the shop's website is www.computerland.co.uk.

What do the initials WWW stand for?

W________________ Wide W________________ — KU 1

KU	PS

7. A factory which manufactures washing machines is planning to use robots to automate their assembly lines.

(*a*) State why the workforce might be concerned about the introduction of the robots. **1**

____

____

(*b*) State an **initial** cost and a **running** cost of installing the robots on the assembly lines. **2**

____

____

____

____

KU	PS

(*c*) Some employees will be working on the assembly lines near the robots. Describe **two** safety precautions that need to be taken. **PS 2**

(*d*) State the part of a robot which allows it to turn around through 360°. **KU 1**

(*e*) State **two** ways in which the robots can increase the productivity of the factory. **PS 2**

8. The Scottish Exam Board uses computers to process the marks achieved by students in the national exams.

	KU	PS
(*a*) (i) When marks are entered into the computer as a percentage, the computer checks that the mark are between 0 and 100. State the type of check used here.		1
(ii) Each student has a candidate number which is always 8 digits long. State how the program can identify errors when a candidate number is entered.		1
(*b*) When an exam mark is entered, the grade awarded automatically appears on the screen. State the name given to this type of processing.	1	
(*c*) A science college contacts the exam board and offers to pay money for a list of students who did well in science subjects. State why the college would want to pay for the student list.		1
(*d*) The exam board uses a broadband connection to access school and university websites. State **two** advantages of a broadband connection over a dial-up connection.	2	

TOTAL MARKS KU...36 PS...36

[End of Question Paper]

Exam C – Credit Paper

Computing Studies Standard Grade: Credit

Practice Papers
For SQA Exams

Credit Level
Exam C

Fill in these boxes:

Name of centre	Town
Forename(s)	**Surname**

You are allowed 1 hour, 45 minutes to complete this paper.

Make sure you read the questions carefully.

Try to answer all of the questions in the time allowed.

Write your answers in the spaces provided.

Make sure you write as neatly as you can and answer in sentences wherever possible.

Leckie × Leckie
Scotland's leading educational publishers

KU	PS

1. The spreadsheet shown below shows a league table for ten football teams after they have all played 7 matches.

Teams are given 3 points for a win, 1 point for a draw and 0 points for a loss.

	A	B	C	D	E	F
1	**Points**					
2	Win	3				
3	Draw	1				
4						
5	**Team**	**Played**	**Won**	**Drew**	**Lost**	**Points**
6	Harrington Rovers	7	6	1	0	19
7	Westwood	7	5	0	2	15
8	Hillston	7	4	2	1	14
9	Kingston	7	3	3	1	12
10	Darrick United	7	3	1	3	10
11	Bullcaster City	7	2	2	3	8
12	Langford	7	2	2	3	8
13	Romford United	7	1	2	4	5
14	Farringdon	7	0	2	5	2
15	Raeburn City	7	0	1	6	1
16						

(*a*) Cell B6 contains a formula which is *replicated* into cells B7 to B15.

(i) State the formula in cell B6. **1** (KU)

____

(ii) State why *relative referencing* is used. **1** (PS)

____

____

(*b*) (i) State what an *absolute reference* is. **1** (KU)

____

____

____

____

(ii) The formula used to calculate the Points for Harrington Rovers in cell F6 is replicated down column F.
State the formula in cell F6. **2** (PS)

____

____

____

	KU	PS

(*c*) (i) The chart shown below was created from the data in the spreadsheet with a dynamic link.

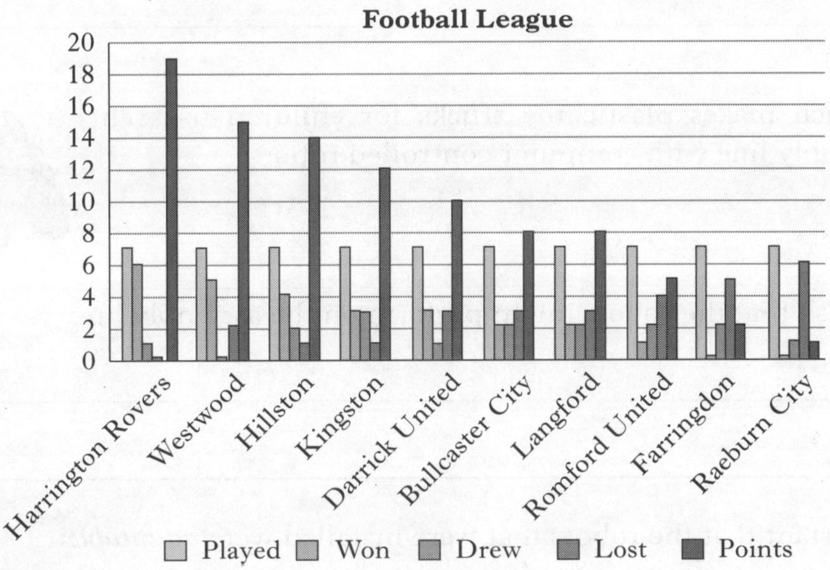

State the effect on the graph above if the points awarded for a win was increased to 4. **1** (PS)

(ii) State why a dynamic link is preferable to a static link in this situation. **1** (PS)

(*d*) The spreadsheet has keyboard shortcuts. **1** (KU)

State one advantage to the user of using keyboard shortcuts.

(*e*) A hardcopy is required of the details of the top three teams in the league. **2** (PS)

State how this can be carried out.

(*f*) Some of the cells in the spreadsheet have been locked so that their contents can't be changed deliberately or by accident.

(i) State the spreadsheet feature which allows this to happen. **1** (KU)

	KU	PS
(ii) State a cell that could have its contents locked and **justify** your answer.		1

2. A company which makes plastic toy trucks for children uses an automated assembly line with computer controlled robots.

	KU	PS
(*a*) State **one** task that the robots might perform on the assembly line.	1	
(*b*) It was important that the robots that were installed were *adaptable*. State what is meant by the term 'adaptable'.	1	
(*c*) State **two** ways in which the design of the workplace would change as a result of automation.		2
(*d*) (i) The programs for the robots were written in a *control language*. State **one** reason why the control language was used.	1	
(ii) The programs were translated into *machine code* by a *compiler*. State **two** advantages of using a compiler over an *interpreter*.	2	

KU	PS

(iii) The programs to control the robots are stored in a ROM chip. State **two** reasons why the programs are stored in ROM. KU 2

____

____

____

____

(*e*) The heating system in the factory is controlled by a computer system that uses temperature *sensors*.

State why this system would require an *A to D converter*. PS 1

____

____

3. A national lottery competition requires the entrants to select 7 numbers. Each number is in the range 1 to 49. The document shown below is used for the numbers to be entered into a computer system.

Lottery Ticket No. 8437336
Date: 250409

1 ☐	2 ☐	3 ☐	4 ☐	5 ☐	6 ☐	7 ☐
8 ☐	9 ☐	10 ☐	11 ☐	12 ☐	13 ☐	14 ☐
15 ☐	16 ☐	17 ☐	18 ☐	19 ☐	20 ☐	21 ☐
22 ☐	23 ☐	24 ☐	25 ☐	26 ☐	27 ☐	28 ☐
29 ☐	30 ☐	31 ☐	32 ☐	33 ☐	34 ☐	35 ☐
36 ☐	37 ☐	38 ☐	39 ☐	40 ☐	41 ☐	42 ☐
43 ☐	44 ☐	45 ☐	46 ☐	47 ☐	48 ☐	49 ☐

(*a*) State the name given to this type of document. KU 1

____

KU	PS

(*b*) State the advantage of using this system to enter the data instead of OCR. — PS 1

(c) (i) Each week over 48 million people enter the lottery.

Choose the computer system most suitable for the lottery to use.

Tick (✓) **one** box only.

Mainframe ☐

Desktop ☐

Laptop ☐ — KU 1

(ii) State a reason for your choice of computer system. — PS 1

(*d*) (i) Each lottery ticket requires 64 bytes of storage.

What are the storage requirements of all 48 million tickets?
(Give your answer in Megabytes) — PS 2

(ii) State a suitable backing store device for the lottery data and **justify** your answer. — PS 2

4. An artist is creating illustrations for a children's book. Each illustration is created in a graphics program in black and white.

An example of one of the images is shown below.

1280 pixels

1200 pixels

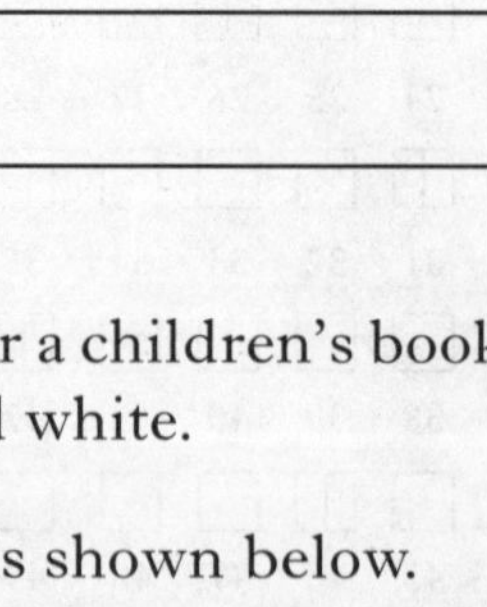

	KU	PS
(*a*) Calculate the storage requirement of this black and white graphic. (Give your answer in kilobytes.)		3
(*b*) (i) State **two** *standard file formats* that could be used to save this file.	2	
(ii) State **one** advantage of saving a file in a standard file format.		1
(*c*) The artist is asked to *crop* some of the graphics. State what it means to crop a graphic.	1	
(*d*) (i) The book was created using a software package which combined text and graphics. State a type of software package appropriate to this task.	1	
(ii) State **two** ways in which the *HCI* of a software package could be customised.		1

5. A zoo has 620 animals and 140 employees. The zoo office has a client/server network of 16 computers which is used to maintain the zoo website and to do administration.

	KU	PS
(*a*) (i) State what is meant by the term "client/server network".	2	

	KU	PS

(ii) State **two** servers that you would expect to find on a client/server network. **2** (KU)

____

____

(iii) State an item of hardware which all computers require to have to be connected to the network. **1** (KU)

____

____

(*b*) The zoo stores details on the animals in a computerised database.

One of the records is shown below.

Field Name	**Data**
Species	Panda
Nickname	Chewey
Sex	Female
Age	6
Diet	Leaves, Shoots
Weight (Kg)	120

Explain how the database can be used to produce a list of elephants that are under 10 years old. **3** (PS)

____

____

____

____

(*c*) The zoo sends out personalised letters to zoo visitors to ask them if they want to sponsor a baby gorilla in the zoo. The letters are created by inserting data held in a database into positions in a standard letter. **1** (KU)

State the name of the process used to create these personalized letters.

____

(*d*) The zoo has a website to display information about the zoo and to attract visitors.

The website is maintained at the zoo using a web page editor.

(i) State **one** reason why a WYSIWYG editor is used instead of HTML to create the web pages. **1** (PS)

____

____

	KU	PS

(ii) The website contains audio and video.
State **two** ways of including audio and video in a web page. — KU 2

(*e*) An expert system is used to help the zoo keepers when animals are sick.
State **two** advantages of using an expert system in this situation. — PS 2

(f) The zoo pays its bills by EFT.

(i) State what the letters EFT stand for. — KU 1

E ______ F ______ T ______

(ii) State **two** advantages of paying bills by EFT. — PS 2

(*g*) The computers on the network are currently connected with transmission cables.

There are plans to move to a *wireless* network.

(i) State **one** advantage of moving to a wireless network. — PS 1

(ii) State **two** ways of accessing the Internet through a *wireless mobile internet technology*. — KU 2

6. Polly wants to buy a new computer. She sees an advert in a newspaper for two computers.

Desktop	**Laptop**
PowerPlusII	**Total D2000**
3 GHz Processor	1.8 GHz Processor
4 Gb RAM	1 Gb RAM
480 Gb Hard Disc Drive	180 Gb Hard Disc Drive
DVD RW Drive	CD ROM Drive

	KU	PS
(*a*) Polly is going to use the computer to create *multimedia* applications.		
(i) State what is meant by the term multimedia.	1	
(ii) State which computer you think is best suited to Polly's needs and **justify** your answer.		2
(*b*) Polly requires to make regular *backups* of the files stored on the computer. Why is the *desktop computer* better than the *laptop* for this purpose?		1
(*c*) State the name given to the type of access used by a hard disk drive?	1	
(*d*) Both of the computers have the same operating system already installed. Describe **two** functions of an operating system.	2	
(*e*) The desktop computer has a *TFT* screen. State what the letters TFT stand for.	1	

T__________ F__________ T__________

7. An Olympic ski team uses a virtual reality simulator to train its downhill racers.

	KU	PS
(*a*) State what is meant by the term virtual reality.	1	
(*b*) State **two** reasons why a virtual reality simulator is used to train the skiers.		2
(*c*) Before the simulator was installed, a systems analyst was called in to help them set up the system. Describe **two** tasks that the systems analyst would have carried out.	2	
(*d*) (i) The team manager keeps a database which holds training data about the skiers. State a piece of legislation which states that the data should be deleted when it is no longer required.	1	
(ii) State another requirement of this act.	1	

TOTAL MARKS **KU…36** **PS…36**

[End of Question Paper]

Worked Answers

1. This question covers aspects of the General Purpose Packages topic and in particular the Word Processing topic. The features of word processing that you have learned in your practical work can be used as a basis for questions that demand written answers in the exam.

1. (*a*) Highlight paragraph 3 and choose the cut option. (**1 mark**)

Move the cursor to just before paragraph 2 and select the paste option. (**1 mark**)

HINT

This type of question very often has more than one way of carrying out the task. The one given here would certainly gain the 2 marks but, equally, you could talk about highlighting paragraph 3 and dragging and dropping it just before paragraph 2.

In a question like this one, where you are asked to explain how to carry out a practical task, try to give an answer that is easy to describe in simple steps.

(*b*) Landscape. (**1 mark**)

(*c*) A standard paragraph is a block of text that has been entered into a computer and saved so that it can be inserted into future documents without the need to re-enter the text. (**1 mark**)

(*d*) On-line help is used when the user needs information on how to carry out a specific task. (**1 mark**)

An on-line tutorial is used to give the user a tour of the main features of a new package. (**1 mark**)

(*e*) Any **two** of the following answers would gain **1 mark** each:

Passwords can be used to restrict access to files. (**1 mark**)

Data can be encrypted (putting data into a code). (**1 mark**)

Physical methods such as locks on doors can be used. (**1 mark**)

(*f*) (i) The client's name is not in the spellcheck dictionary. (**1 mark**)

(ii) The client's name can be added to the dictionary. (**1 mark**)

(iii) Any **two** of the following answers would gain **1 mark** each:

No capital letter at the start of a sentence. (**1 mark**)

Using the wrong tense of a verb. (**1 mark**)

Using a plural when a singular is expected. (**1 mark**)

TOP EXAM TIP

One issue in the exam is to know how much to write. Each question has a space provided for your answer so obviously the amount of space is a good indication of how much you should write. The problem with this is that different students have different sizes of handwriting, so you should consider the size of your own handwriting in judging how much to write.

Another important factor is the amount of marks allocated to the question. If a question is worth 2 marks then you are expected to make 2 points in your answer.

In general, if you are using up less than half of the available space then you probably are not giving enough detail and explanation in your answers.

2. This question covers most of the content of the graphics topic at General level. Cropping a graphic is only asked for at Credit level but you need to know about scaling and editing graphics for General level.

2. (*a*) Any one of the following answers would gain **1 mark**:

The fill colour has been changed. (**1 mark**)

The outline thickness has been changed. (**1 mark**)

(*b*) Any one of the following answers would gain **1 mark**:

A pen tool. (**1 mark**)

A rubber tool. (**1 mark**)

A paint spray tool. (**1 mark**)

HINT These are only some of the possible answers. Any tool that is used to alter the colour of individual pixels would be found in a painting package but not in a drawing package which works with shapes and not pixels.

(*c*) Scaling a graphic is to enlarge or reduce it. (**1 mark**)

(*d*) The graphic has been rotated 90° clockwise. (**1 mark**)

HINT To say that the graphic has been rotated 270° anti-clockwise is an equally correct answer.

(*e*) Text. (**1 mark**)

3. Commercial data processing is one of the biggest topics in the Standard Grade Computing Studies course. You can expect to get several marks allocated to this topic in both the General and the Credit exams.

3. (*a*) A mark sense card. (**1 mark**)

(*b*) Any **one** of the following answers would gain **1 mark**:

The possibility of a human typing in the wrong data is eliminated by entering the data directly from the card. (**1 mark**)

The data can be read in quicker from the card than a human could type the data in. (**1 mark**)

(*c*) A systems analyst observes and analyses a system. (**1 mark**)

Advises upon which hardware and software is required to implement a computerised system. (**1 mark**)

TOP EXAM TIP

It is better to include any relevant technical terms in your answers where appropriate. For example, when asked to describe the type of access on a hard disk drive, the first answer given below is better than the second answer, which does not use the term direct/random access.

Answer 1

"A hard disk uses direct/random access. This is fast access since the data can be accessed directly from any point on the storage device."

Answer 2

"A hard disk has fast access since the data can be accessed directly from any point on the storage device."

(*d*) Cost of paper for the forms, ink for the printers, hardware maintenance, electricity, etc. (**1 mark**)

(*e*) Data is the raw facts stored on a computer system. Information is data once it has been given meaning. (**1 mark**)

HINT The difference between data and information can be expressed by the equation: INFORMATION = DATA + MEANING

(*f*) (i) Any **one** of the following answers would gain **1 mark**:

Goods are generally cheaper. (**1 mark**)

There is a global market to choose from. (**1 mark**)

You can shop 24/7. (**1 mark**)

(ii) Any **one** of the following answers would gain **1 mark**:

There is a danger of credit card fraud. (**1 mark**)

You can't touch or see the goods close up to inspect the quality. (**1 mark**)

(*g*) Magnetic Ink Character Recognition. (**1 mark**)

4. Stationary and mobile robots are covered in this question together with the social impact of automating factories and assembly lines.

4. (*a*) Yaw movements are performed by the wrist. (**1 mark**)

The wrist moves from side to side in a yaw movement. (**1 mark**)

(*b*) Any **one** of the following answers would gain **2 marks**:

Painting car parts (**1 mark**) with a paint spray gun. (**1 mark**)
Weld car parts together (**1 mark**) with a welder. (**1 mark**)
Lift car parts into place (**1 mark**) with a gripper. (**1 mark**)

(*c*) Any **one** of the following answers would gain **2 marks**:

White lines are painted on the floor and the robot shines a light on the floor which is reflected best by the white line. (**1 mark**) A light sensor on the robot detects if the robot is over the white line or not. (**1 mark**)

Electrical wires are buried just under the floor which generate a magnetic field. (**1 mark**) A magnetic field sensor on the robot detects if the robot is over the wire or not. (**1 mark**)

HINT There are of course lots of other means of guiding a mobile robot around a floor. Pupils often come up with railway tracks and so on. For the purpose of this course you must not do this and restrict your answer to white lines or electrical wires.

(*d*) Any **one** of the following answers would gain **1 mark**:

Workers could write the programs to run the robots. (**1 mark**)

They could maintain and repair the robots. (**1 mark**)

(*e*) Any **one** of the following advantages would gain **1 mark**:

They can word in dirty and hazardous environments. (**1 mark**)

Robots can work 24/7 and do not go on strike. (**1 mark**)

They are more accurate and consistent than a human. (**1 mark**)

Any **one** of the following disadvantages would gain **1 mark**:

Humans are made unemployed as a result of using robots. (**1 mark**)

Robots do not have the ability to adapt and show common sense. (**1 mark**)

> **5.** This question covers sorting and searching databases. These types of questions are repeated in later papers in this book because they are often answered badly in the exam. Make sure that you know how to answer these questions.

5. (*a*) Best Break. (**1 mark**)

> *HINT* It is a common mistake to think that fields such as the Date of Birth field or the Telephone Number field are numeric fields. These are not numeric fields since the data they hold is not treated as a quantity and can't be used in calculations.

(*b*) A new field has to be inserted called something like Team Player (**1 mark**) and the data "Yes" or "No" entered for each player. (**1 mark**)

(*c*) Sort the database on the Best Break field (**1 mark**) in descending order and the first record will be the highest best break. (**1 mark**)

> *HINT* It is possible to answer this question by searching for records where the Best Break field is over a certain value, to select a subset of the records and then search again to home in on the highest best break. This would certainly work but it is not as efficient as sorting the records into ascending or descending order. When asked to find the highest or smallest value in a field, always give an answer that uses a sort.

(*d*) Perform a complex *Search* (**1 mark**) where the *Sex* (**1 mark**) field equals "Female" *AND* (**1 mark**) the Date of Birth field *Is greater than* (**1 mark**) 01/04/95.

> *HINT* This is a very common type of exam question. In the General paper you will probably be given a paragraph to insert the correct words chosen from a list. However in the Credit paper you will have to come up with the entire answer by yourself.

> **6.** This question covers aspects of spreadsheets at General level. You will not be asked about absolute cell references, relative cell references and the IF function at this level.

6. (*a*) (i) I4. (**1 mark**)

(ii) =SUM(B4:H4). (**1 mark**)

> *HINT* Using the SUM function is more efficient when adding up a large number of cells.

(*b*) =MAX(B4:H4). (**2 marks**)

> **HINT** 1 mark is awarded for stating that a MAX function is required and 1 mark is awarded for the correct range of cells.

(*c*) Replication is where a formula is copied either across a row or down a column or filled down or filled across to other cells. (**1 mark**)

(*d*) Column A should be made wider. (**1 mark**)

> **HINT** The size of a cell is described by its height and width. It is better to say the cell is made wider than to be too general by stating something like it has been made bigger or fatter.

(*e*) Highlight the cells from A3 to H4. (**1 mark**) Select the pie chart option from the charting menu. (**1 mark**)

> **7.** This question covers the content of several chapters though the scenario of a person working from home. The General Purpose Packages, Internet and Hardware chapters are examined.

7. (*a*) Teleworking. (**1 mark**)

(*b*) Jasper would use a word processor program. (**1 mark**)

(*c*) The computer that Jasper bought was Internet ready with *browser* software already installed and it had a *modem* to transmit data from the computer down the telephone line.

Jasper opted for a *broadband* connection for its fast speed.

(3 × 1 mark is awarded for each correct word.)

> **TOP EXAM TIP**
> The examiner's report states that students often leave gaps in questions where a tick or choosing a word or term to fill a blank in a paragraph could gain a mark. Make sure that you answer all questions and give yourself a chance of a mark even if you are guessing.

(*d*) (i) An inkjet printer.

An inkjet printer is cheaper than a laser printer and the faster printing speed of a laser printer is not required for one person. (**1 mark**)

> **HINT** In this type of question where you are asked to justify your choice one answer is usually expected but another will be accepted provided that you give a good reason for your choice.

(ii) A wizard is a step by step guide through an unfamiliar task. (**1 mark**)

(*e*) Any one of: a digital camera, a scanner, a mobile phone, a webcam. (**1 mark**)

> **HINT** It is important to say **digital** camera. It a common mistake for students to just say camera which will not gain a mark.

(*f*) The tick should be in the Data file box. (**1 mark**)

> **HINT** Always answer this type of question even if it has to be a guess. You will not lose any marks for a wrong answer.

(*g*) Jasper should group his files in folders/directories on the hard disc.

> **TOP EXAM TIP**
> It is important that you read the text at the start of a question which sets the context for the question. This is not put here for decoration but has a strong bearing on what you should write in your answer. For example, if a question mentions in the preamble that a computer user has poor eyesight and asks how the human computer interface might be customised then you should talk about making the icons larger and activating sound alerts rather than general points such as customising toolbars and changing the font in menus.

8. This question covers some of the content of the Low Level Machine chapter at General level. This chapter can often require a calculator to work out the answers so make sure that you have a working one in the exam.

8. (*a*) (i) Eight. (**1 mark**)

(ii) Machine Code is the computer's own language using binary codes to represent instructions and data. (**1 mark**)

HINT Question which ask you to state or name something do not need to be answered in sentences. It will not improve your answer in any way to say "There are eight bits in a byte." However a question that asks for an explanation or a description can't be answered in one work or term and you must answer in sentences.

(*b*) Disc capacity = 1.4 Megabytes = 1.4 × 1,024 = 1,433.6 Kilobytes. (**1 mark**)

The free space on the disc = 1,433.6 – 424 – 916 = 93.6 Kilobytes. (**1 mark**)

HINT It is important to show the working in calculation questions such as this.

(*c*)

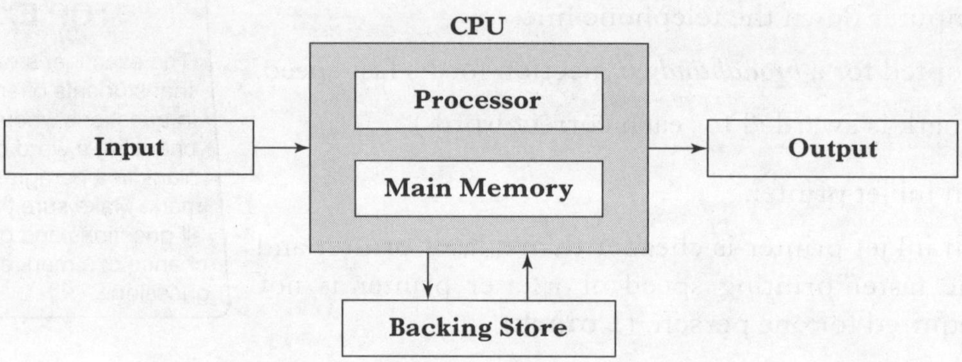

(3 × 1 mark is awarded for each correct word/term.)

(*d*) Text is represented on a computer system by using an 8 bit code called an ASCII code. (American Standard Code for Information Interchange) for each character. (**1 mark**)

HINT There are other standards for representing text on a computer system but you should talk about ASCII for this course.

(*e*) ROM (Read Only Memory). (**1 mark**)

1. This question covers commonly asked concepts on general purpose packages. It addresses the important concept of static and dynamic links and features of word processing and spreadsheet packages.

1. (*a*) A spreadsheet. (**1 mark**)

HINT: A spreadsheet is better than other general purpose packages such as a database and word processing software because it has formula and functions to perform calculations and has a charting facility.

(*b*) A title for the chart. (**1 mark**)

A label for the *x*-axis or the *y*-axis. (**1 mark**)

(*c*) A dynamic link should be used between the spreadsheet and the bar chart. (**1 mark**) The data is constantly changing and the bar graph will be automatically updated as the data changes. (**1 mark**)

HINT: If a static link had been used then the bar graph would not automatically change when the data in the spreadsheet changes.

TOP EXAM TIP

Questions that ask you to state an item of software for your answer expect you to give a general term for the application and not a commercial product. For example, in this question you should say a spreadsheet and not Microsoft Excel. This principal applies to other general purpose packages in that you should use terms such as word processing, database, graphics. etc. and not Word, Access, Photoshop, etc. The examiner's report has stated quite clearly that you will not gain any marks if you do not take this advice.

(*d*) A printer driver. (**1 mark**) This is an item of software that allows the computer to communicate with a printer. (**1 mark**)

HINT: It is a common mistake to state that a printer driver connects a computer to a printer. This is not detailed enough since it does not mention that it is an item of software or what it does.

(e) (i) Data subjects have the right to see what data is being held on them apart from the police and national security organisations. (**1 mark**)

They can also insist that inaccuracies in their data are corrected. (**1 mark**)

HINT: A third answer here is to state that data that is no longer required when a person leaves an organisation should be deleted.

(ii) A The Copyright, Designs and Patents Act. (**1 mark**)

B The Computer Misuse Act (1990). (**1 mark**)

(*f*) The data is presented clearly in rows and columns and can be formatted to look attractive with different cell fill colours, border line patterns and so on. (**1 mark**)

It is easy to insert extra rows and columns to enter more data. (**1 mark**)

HINT: A possible third answer here could be that the text in the cells will stay together as a unit if the table is moved.

(*g*) Search and replace. (**1 mark**)

HINT Some work processing software describe search and replace as "find and change". This answer is equally acceptable.

(*h*) A template is a document with some content and structure already in place that is used over and over again as the basis for new documents. **(1 mark)**

2. This is a typical spreadsheet question in a Credit paper. It covers key areas of this topic, such as absolute and relative cell referencing, and standard functions, such as SUM and IF.

There will certainly be quite a few marks awarded to spreadsheet questions in the exam.

2. (*a*) B2. **(1 mark)**

HINT Any other cell containing money is correct. Cells F5 to F8 and G5 to G8 are also correct.

(*b*) =SUM(B5:E5). **(1 mark)**

HINT An alternative answer is to use the formula =B5 + C5 + D5 + E5 which would gain the marks. However it is better to use the SUM function since it is more efficient, especially with a large number of cells to add up.

(*c*) Relative cell referencing. **(1 mark)**

When the formula is filled down the column, the cells have to change for each row to make the formula correct and not stay the same, which would be absolute cell referencing. **(1 mark)**

(*d*) (i) = $B$2 * F5 **(2 marks)**

HINT "1 mark is given for the correct formula and the second mark for making B2 an absulute cell reference."

(ii) B2 contains the price of the book and this must stay the same for each formula in column G when the formula in G5 is filled down. **(1 mark)**

(e) = IF (F5 < 200, "Poor", "OK"). **(3 marks)**

HINT 1 mark is given for the IF function, 1 mark for the condition "F5 < 200" and 1 mark for the text "OK"

There has been a pattern of asking this type of question in recent years in the exam so make sure that you know the format of the IF function.

TOP EXAM TIP

An IF function is also known as a conditional function.

3. This question requires the use of a calculator. There is usually a need for the use of a calculator in one or two questions in the exam.

3. (*a*) A scanner can be used to input the graphic into a computer. **(1 mark)**

The graphic file is then sent as an attachment with an e-mail. **(1 mark)**

HINT It is important to state that the graphic file is sent as an **attachment** with an e-mail and not just that it is e-mailed.

(*b*) (i) A standard file can be recognised and opened by any graphics program and not just the particular graphics program that was used to create it. (**1 mark**)

(ii) GIF (Graphics Interchange Format) or JPEG (Joint Photographic Expert Group). (**1 mark**)

HINT There are other standard file formats for graphics but either GIF or JPEG are good answers for this course.

(c) The graphic has 2,400 × 1,280 = 3,072,000 pixels.

Each pixel requires 1 bit of storage = 3,072,000 bits. (**1 mark**)

3,072,000/8 (**1 mark**) = 384,000 bytes = 384,000/1024 (**1 mark**) = 375 Kb.

HINT The common mistake in working out the capacity of black and white graphics is to use 2 bits per pixel instead of 1 bit. Only 1 bit is required per pixel since it has two possible states (1 for black and 0 for white.)

(*d*) (i) The remaining space on the USB flash is 2Mb = 2 × 1,024 Kb = 2,048 Kb. (**1 mark**)

The file is only 375 Kb and so can be saved on the USB flash. (**1 mark**)

(ii) USB flash is more portable than a CD disc or USB flash is more robust than a CD. (**1 mark**)

TOP EXAM TIP

If you make a mistake in the calculation for the first part of a calculation question you can still gain all the marks for the second part, provided you show working to support a correct understanding of the second part. The marker will not keep taking off marks for the first mistake.

4. This is a very common type of question on databases. It covers the key areas of selecting records, computed fields and how a database is used in mail merge. If you can understand the answers to this question then you should be able to answer similar questions in your own exam.

4. (*a*) The data can be validated by the program rejecting any data (**1 mark**) other than a "F" or a "M". (**1 mark**)

HINT It is a common mistake for pupils to confuse validation with verification. Validation is where the software asks for data that is not possible to be entered again. Verification is where the same data is entered twice and any differences between the two items of data are highlighted and corrected.

(*b*) Perform a complex search to select the records where the Sex field = "F" (**1 mark**) and the Town field = "Edinburgh". (**1 mark**) Finally produce a printout of the selected records. (**1 mark**)

HINT This is a very common exam question where you are asked to select records in a database. You must specify the field names and the values that they are required to take. It is a common mistake to give an answer such as "Go to the database and get the authors who are female and live in Edinburgh." which will gain no marks.

(*c*) Step 1
Create letter. (**1 mark**)

Step 2
Create datafile (**1 mark**)

Step 3
Mail merge. (**1 mark**)

(*d*) (i) A computed field is a field whose data is calculated from other fields in a record using a formula. (**1 mark**)

(ii) The data in the computed field is worked out automatically from a formula (**1 mark**) so that there is no need to spend time entering the data manually. (**1 mark**)

HINT A large number of students lose marks in the exam by not knowing what is meant by a computed field. This type of question is quite common so make sure that you know what a computed field is and its use in databases.

5. Automated systems include the study of stationary and mobile robots so this question has been written to address issues relating to both of these robots. Watch out for the use of a ROM chip to store the robot's program and control language in this area of the course.

5. (*a*) The electricity bill might increase because robots need a lot of electricity to be powered. (**1 mark**)

The electricity bill might go down because with fewer human workers the warehouse would need less heating and lighting. (**1 mark**)

(*b*) (i) An intelligent robot is one that can adapt its actions according to changes in its environment. (**1 mark**)

(ii) Sensors. (**1 mark**)

HINT Sensors allow a robot to adapt to its environment by sending feedback signals to the controlling computer about what is happening about it.

(*c*) (i) The program can't be deleted or overwritten. (**1 mark**)

The ROM chip keeps its contents when power is switched off. (**1 mark**)

(ii) A control language is a high level language that uses English command words and instructions specific to the control of the robots. (**1 mark**)

(*d*) The light sensors would have difficulty in sensing the light emitted from the white lines if the floor was dirty but the magnetic field from electric wires would not be affected. (**1 mark**)

HINT Mobile robots find their way around an area by either by using light sensors to follow white lines or magnetic field sensors to follow electric wires on the floor.

TOP EXAM TIP

Take care in your spelling and the neatness of your answers in the exam.

The front of the exam paper has the instruction "Write as neatly as possible."

Obviously you do not want to write too slowly for the sake of neatness that you struggle to finish the exam. On the other hand, if your writing is so messy that the examiner finds it difficult to work out what you have written or it is completely illegible then you will certainly lose marks.

If you have learning difficulties and are allowed a scribe in the exam then you will not have to worry about spelling, grammar and neatness (hopefully)!

6. Features of high level languages and their translators (interpreters and compilers) are regularly asked so this question gives you practice in this area of the course.

6. (*a*) Any **two** of the following answers would gain **1 mark** each:

They use English command words. **(1 mark)**

Complex arithmetical operations can be performed in one instruction. **(1 mark)**

One High Level Language instruction translates into many Machine Code instructions. **(1 mark)**

They have inbuilt functions to perform mathematical and logical processing of the data. **(1 mark)**

The program can be broken down into procedures. **(1 mark)**

(*b*) An interpreter. **(1 mark)**

An interpreted language is better than a compiled language at amending a program because it translates one instruction at a time at run time and will stop at an error, which can then be corrected and the program can be run again without delay. **(1 mark)**

HINT The differences between a compiler and an interpreter are extremely common exam questions so make sure that you know how they both operate and their differences.

(*c*) Portable means how easy a program can be adapted to run on a different computer system from the one for which it was originally written. **(1 mark)**

HINT Low Level Language programs are less portable than High Level Language programs since the Low Level Language instructions are specific to one computer system.

(*d*) Foreground/Background Printing is where the processor is shared between the foreground task of dealing with input from the user and the background task of sending data to the printer. **(1 mark)**

The user can continue to use the computer while printing goes on in the background. **(1 mark)**

7. This question addresses networks and wireless networking. Wireless networking is becoming more and more popular in homes and offices and, to reflect this, there has been an increase in the number of marks given to this topic in the exam.

7. (*a*) NIC (Network Interface Card). **(1 mark)**

(*b*) A file server stores and controls access to programs and users' files on a network. **(1 mark)**

TOP EXAM TIP

There are lots of acronyms in computing such as RAM (Random Access Memory), ALU (Arithmetic Logic Unit), and so on. You will probably be asked to say what a few of them stand for in the exam so learn them all.

HINT Students are very often too vague in describing the function of a file server. You need to write something close to the answer above and not something along the lines of "A file server keeps the data."

(*c*) Any **one** of the following answers would gain the marks:

The ALU (**1 mark**) performs arithmetic operations such as adding and subtracting and logical operations such as AND and OR. (**1 mark**)

Registers (**1 mark**) are single storage locations within the CPU that are used to store items of data that the processor is actively working on. (**1 mark**)

HINT This is one of the most frequently asked questions in the Computer System area of the course. LEARN a good description of the **three** components of the processor. i.e. The control unit, ALU and register.

(*d*) (i) Wireless networking allows the computers to be moved around more freely in a less cluttered environment / they have no cables / they can receive the Internet anywhere. (**1 mark**)

(ii) Wireless networking operates at slower speeds than conventional cabling. (**1 mark**)

8. This question covers the topics of the Internet and Web Page Creation.
These are quite short topics and are often integrated into one question.

8. (*a*) HTML (Hypertext Markup Language). (**1 mark**)

(*b*) The images can be captured with a digital camera (**1 mark**) and a scanner. (**1 mark**)

HINT Technically the images could be captured using a scanner but the images would need to be available on paper. It is hard to use a scanner to capture an image of a live author! It is best to say digital camera for this type of question.

(*c*) Any **one** of the following answers would gain **1 mark**:

They could use sound to give a description of the book. (**1 mark**)

They could use sound effects for an action book. (**1 mark**)

They could use a video of an author talking about his book. (**1 mark**)

(*d*) Shareware. (**1 mark**)

HINT There are **three** types of software that can be downloaded from the Internet: Freeware, shareware and commercial software. These are all commonly asked for in the exam.

1. This question brings together several topics but mainly examines key points in the commercial data processing chapter.

1. (*a*) A mainframe computer is required because it can store the large volume of data required in CDP. (**1 mark**)

An expensive, powerful computer is needed to process the large amounts of data. (**1 mark**)

(*b*) MICR is a special magnetic ink which is difficult to forge. (**1 mark**)

(*c*) (i) Electronic Funds Transfer. (**1 mark**)

HINT This is a very common type of exam question where you are asked to state what the initials of a term stand for.

(ii) A check digit is added to the barcode. (**1 mark**)

(*d*) (i) Hard disk. (**1 mark**)

HINT A hard disk is required for its high capacity and fast direct access. A floppy disk does not store enough data and magnetic tape has slow sequential access.

(ii) Touch sensitive screens are very user friendly so that people with little computing skills will find it easy to use. (**1 mark**)

(*e*) Pages Per Minute. (PPM) (**1 mark**)

(*f*) (i) Any **one** of the following answers would gain a mark.

They could check how much money they have in their account. (**1 mark**)

They could pay for bills. (**1 mark**)

They could order a new chequebook. (**1 mark**)

NB. There are lots of other reasonable answers to this question.

(ii) They might be worried about security of their account details. (**1 mark**)

2. This question examines word processing. Candidates usually find this to be a fairly easy topic because it is the general purpose package that they have the most experience of.

2 (a) Landscape. (**1 mark**)

HINT There are two types of page layout used in word processing. These are portrait and landscape.

(*b*) Any **one** of the following answers would gain a mark.

It is easy to insert new rows and columns to incorporate new data. **(1 mark)**

Formatting can be applied to the cells in the table. **(1 mark)**

There are too many answers to list here. If you are not sure ask your teacher for advice.

(*c*) The cell has been centre aligned. **(1 mark)**

HINT Left, right and centre alignment can also be described as left, right and centre justification although the term justification is used less frequently in this course.

(*d*) A new row can be inserted into the table to incorporate the new booking time above the 12.00 – 13.00 row. **(1 mark)**

(*e*) (i) A database package. **(1 mark)**
(ii) Records can be selected quickly. **(1 mark)**
The records can be sorted into different orders. **(1 mark)**

HINT A common mistake in this question would be to give the reason that the data can be easily edited or that it saves paper. Of course, these are advantages of holding data on computer but they are not reasons why a database is more suited than a spreadsheet or a word processing program.

(*f*) (i) Windows Icons Menu Pointer. **(1 mark)**
(ii) A WIMP interface improves the user friendliness of a computer / makes it easier for a beginner to use the computer. **(1 mark)**

TOP EXAM TIP

There has been some confusion of what WIMP stands for. Some sources will describe WIMP as Windows, Icons, Mouse, Pull down menus. The exam board has made it clear that Windows, Icons, Menu, Pointer is the only description that they will accept in this course.

(*g*) This is breaking the netiquette rule of shouting. **(1 mark)**

HINT Shouting is a term to describe an e-mail that is written in all capitals.

3. Most students enjoy graphics practical work and questions but make sure that you know the required technical terms and information to answer the exam questions. This question is a typical General level question on this topic.

3. (*a*) Each pixel of the graphic is stored in one bit. A 1 can be used to represent black and a 0 used to represent white. **(1 mark)**

HINT You will only be asked questions on black and white graphics in this course. Colour graphics are examined at higher level.

(*b*) Scale the guitar graphic to reduce its size. **(1 mark)**

Copy and paste the guitar player. **(1 mark)**

Flip the copied image horizontally and position it to the left of the first image. **(1 mark)**

HINT — This question requires three steps to give a full answer but the steps could have been given in a different order and still gain the marks.

(*c*) To rotate a graphic is to turn it through an angle. **(1 mark)**

(*d*) Any **two** of the following answers would gain a mark each.

The line thickness. **(1 mark)**

The line colour. **(1 mark)**

The line pattern. **(1 mark)**

HINT — Lots of students answer this question by describing the position of the line or the length of the line. These are sort of OK but the marker is really looking for the answers given above.

(*e*) An individual graphics program will be more powerful and have more features than one that is part of an integrated package. **(1 mark)**

4. You can expect a spreadsheet question in the General exam at this level of difficulty.

The SUM, MIN, MAX and AVERAGE functions are regularly examined in this topic.

4. (*a*) A spreadsheet. **(1 mark)**

(*b*) Cell B5. **(1 mark)**

HINT — You should give the address of the cell in this question. You probably will not gain a mark by saying that it is the cell to the right of the cell containing Worst Score.

(*c*) The formula is =SUM(B2:G2)-B4-B5

This question could also have been answered correctly with the formula =B2+C2+D2+E2+G2-B4-B5 but it is less efficient.

(*d*) Any **two** of the following answers would gain a mark each.

A1 is left aligned and B1 is centre aligned. **(1 mark)**

A1 is wider than B1. **(1 mark)**

A1 has its text formatted to bold and B1 is in italic text. **(1 mark)**

(*e*) The cell attributes of cell F2 can be changed to 1 decimal place. **(1 mark)**

(*f*) This feature is called cell protection. **(1 mark)**

TOP EXAM TIP

The General exam has a total 72 marks and lasts for 75 minutes. This means that you can spend about 1 minute per mark on a question. Use this as a guide in the exam so that you do not spend too much or too little on each question.

5. This question is on the important database topic. Database questions are fairly predictable in that they usually involve sorting and searching databases amongst other things. You will find that all of the database questions in these papers examine these areas.

5. (*a*) The field types used are text (**1 mark**) and numeric (**1 mark**).

HINT Other field types used in databases are date fields, time fields and graphic fields.

(*b*) A new field can be inserted (**1 mark**) which holds the data "Yes" or "No" depending on whether the shoe is in stock or not. (**1 mark**)

HINT It is better to use the term inserted here rather than simply to say added.

(*c*) Sort the records on the Price (£) field (**1 mark**) in descending order (**1 mark**).

HINT You must mention SORT, the field to sort on and whether it is in ascending or descending order

(*d*) Perform a complex *search* (**1 mark**) where the Age Group field equals *Children* (**1 mark**) AND the Size field *equals* (**1 mark**) 6.

(*e*) The database file requires 640 × 120 bytes of storage. (**1 mark**)

= 76,800 bytes = 76,800 / 1,024 Kilobytes = 75 Kb. (**1 mark**)

HINT Show the working in any calculation question.

6. This question concerns the Internet and computer networks. This area has become more important since 2006 when the Standard Grade course was updated to reflect changes in the use of IT over the past decade.

6. (*a*) (i) Local Area Network. (**1 mark**)

(ii) Wide Area Network (WAN). (**1 mark**)

(*b*) A printer. (**1 mark**)

HINT Other peripheral devices such as scanners and digital cameras could be mentioned here but a printer is the most obvious and best answer.

(*c*) Protect files with user names and passwords. (**1 mark**)

Use encryption to code data. (**1 mark**)

Physical security measures such as locks on doors and keyboards. (**1 mark**)

(*d*) (i) HTML (Hypertext Markup Language). (**1 mark**)

(ii) The customers could use a search engine (**1 mark**) and enter keywords such as "Dumfries", "Flowers" and "shop". (**1 mark**)

(*e*) A computer engineer maintains, upgrades and repairs the hardware of a computer system. (**1 mark**)

TOP EXAM TIP

Pick one of these exam papers and do it under exam conditions. This will be a good way to make sure that you are pacing yourself well before you sit the real exam. Also use the answers to check on your success and to identify what areas you need to work on.

7. This question examines the Hardware and Low Level Machine chapters. Part (*a*) is a type of question common in the General exam where you have to insert words from a list into gaps in a paragraph.

7. (*a*) A *laptop* (**1 mark**) and a desktop computer have QWERTY keyboards to enter data, whereas a *palmtop* (**1 mark**) computer uses a *stylus* (**1 mark**) to write on a *touch sensitive* (**1 mark**) screen. A desktop computer is less *portable* (**1 mark**) than the other two types of computer but usually has a large *TFT* (**1 mark**) screen display.

HINT — This sort of question has not been asked for in the exam recently but it is certainly part of the course and you should be able to answer it.

(*b*) (i) Machine code. (**1 mark**)

(ii) Any **two** of the following answers would gain a mark each.
They use English command words. (**1 mark**)
Complex arithmetical operations can be performed in one instruction. (**1 mark**)
They have inbuilt functions to process the data. (**1 mark**)
The program can be broken down into procedures. (**1 mark**)

HINT — There are other answers to this question but these are the standard ones.

(*c*) A program which manages the hardware of a computer system. (**1 mark**)

(*d*) A directory is an area on a disc (folder) where files are stored. (**1 mark**)

8. This question covers the topic of virtual reality and simulators and the advantage of such systems.

8. (*a*) (i) A real time system is one where data is entered and processed without any time delay because speed of response is vital. (**1 mark**)

(ii) The simulator requires to respond instantly to any input from the pilot so that the system can immediately update the screen display, aircraft speed, etc. (**1 mark**)

(*b*) Any **two** of the following answers would gain **1 mark** each:

Money will be saved as airplane crashes will not happen. (**1 mark**)

Money is saved on fuel and oil. (**1 mark**)

Wear and tear on aircraft parts is avoided. (**1 mark**)

PRACTICE EXAM B — CREDIT LEVEL WORKED ANSWERS

1. This question integrates work from the General Purpose Packages, Internet and Hardware topics. You can expect to be given questions that cover several topics in your own exam.

1. (*a*) (i) A hard disk. **(1 mark)**

A hard disk has a high capacity and *direct/random access* which gives the fast access required to answer telephone inquiries in seconds. **(1 mark)**

HINT Other backing store devices are not suitable because they do not have enough storage space or slow access.

(ii) The records in a database can be searched to meet the criteria of the people **(1 mark)** and can be sorted into order of price, etc. **(1 mark)**

(*b*) Any **one** of the following would gain **1 mark**:

The font size in menus and windows can be made larger. **(1 mark)**

The icons can be made enlarged. **(1 mark)**

Different sounds can be attached to events such as deleting a file. **(1 mark)**

HINT There are lots of other possible answers to this question but the ones given would be the sort of thing that the marker is looking for.

(*c*) (i) A broadband connection is faster than a dial-up connection. **(1 mark)**

A broadband connection is always on / they can use the telephone at the same time / better download speeds. **(1 mark)**

(ii) Netiquette is rules of good behaviour when communicating by e-mail. **(1 mark)**

(*d*) Templates improve productivity because they are the basis of a document with some content and formatting already in place so that the user does not need to start from a blank document. **(1 mark)**

HINT Learn a good definition of the term template. Candidates seem to understand what a template is but are very clumsy at providing a description.

(*e*) A printer driver is an item of software that allows the computer to communicate with he printer. **(1 mark)**

2. You can expect to get quite a few marks on databases in the exam. The question below is designed to prepare you for the most commonly asked questions on this topic.

2. (*a*) One record requires 5 + 20 + 20 + 30 + 20 + 7 + 11 + 1 + 6 = 120 bytes of storage. **(1 mark)**

To store all the record requires 120 × 680 = 81,600 bytes. **(1 mark)**

> **HINT**
>
> A common pitfall is for a student not to provide any working to show how the answer was calculated.
>
> For example, the answer shown below would gain 0 marks.
>
> 76,840.
>
> The student has added up the bytes wrongly and got 113 bytes for one record by missing out the 7 bytes for the Postcode field and had then correctly multiplied the answer by 680 to get 76,840 bytes.
>
> However, because no working was shown then no marks can be awarded.
>
> Also the student has not put the units "bytes" in the answer which would not lose marks but shows a lack of care and attention to detail.
>
> If the student had given the following answer then 1 mark could have been given for the part that was done correctly.
>
> One record requires 5 + 20 + 20 + 30 + 20 + 11 + 1 + 6 = 113 bytes of storage.
>
> To store all the record requires 113 × 680 = 76,840 bytes.

(*b*) (i) A text field. **(1 mark)**

(ii) A date field. **(1 mark)**

> **HINT**
>
> Although the data field is storing six numbers, it is better to store it as a date field rather than a numeric field so that the database software can treat it as a date.

> **TOP EXAM TIP**
>
> A few of the questions in the exam require you to make some fairly simple calculations. You are allowed to use a calculator in the exam so the problem is not getting the right answer to a sum but making sure that you are doing the right sum.
>
> The main things to watch out for here are:
>
> - Show all the working to get the answer.
> - Show any units that apply to your answer such as Kb.

(*c*) A complex search is used to select the records where the Sex field = "M" **(1 mark)** AND the Town field = "Edinburgh". **(1 mark)**

(*d*) A computed field **or** a calculated field. **(1 mark)**

> **HINT**
>
> A computed field is also known as a calculation field but it's better to use computed since it is the term used in the course arrangements document.

(*e*) The input format can be changed to show only a few fields in order to identify the pupil such as Firstname, Surname and code together with the Telephone No. field. **(1 mark)**

The records could be displayed in rows so that the telephone numbers can be easily entered down one column. **(1 mark)**

(*f*) Verification involves the same data being entered twice so that any differences between the two versions caused by errors can be identified and removed. **(1 mark)**

Validation involves the software rejecting data that is not possible and asking for the data to be re-entered. **(1 mark)**

> **HINT**
>
> The difference between verification and validation has been asked for several times in the exam so make sure that you know the difference between them.

(*g*) Four fields have been selected for the output (Firstname, Surname, Sex and Telephone no.) which have been displayed in columnar format. **(1 mark)**

A complex sort has been performed on the records. The first field for the sort is the Sex field in ascending order and the second field for the sort is the Surname field in ascending order. **(1 mark)**

HINT

Students often get confused with what is meant by ascending and descending order in this type of question. Ascending is going up the way which for numbers means getting larger and for letters means A…Z. Descending is going down the way which for numbers means getting smaller and for letters means Z…A.

(*h*) The Computer Misuse Act (1990). **(1 mark)**

HINT

It is a common mistake to mix up the Data Protection Act with the Computer Misuse Act. The Computer Misuse Act is to do with hacking and sending viruses but the Data Protection Act is to do with the rights of individuals that data, held about them on computer systems, is used properly.

3. This question covers the main aspects of Credit level graphics questions. Look out for the calculation of the storage requirements of a black and white graphic.

3. (*a*) The total number of pixels in the graphic = 500 × 240 = 120,000 pixels.

Each pixel in a black and white graphic requires one bit to store so the storage = 120,000 bits. **(1 mark)**

The number of bytes = 120,000/8 = 15,000 bytes. **(1 mark)**

HINT

A student that provides the following answer still gains 1 mark. This is because there is only one mistake in thinking that black and white graphics take 2 bits of storage per pixel and not 1 bit:

The total number of pixels in the graphic = 500 × 240 = 120,000 pixels.

= 120,000 × 2 = 240,000 bits.

The number of bytes = 240,000 / 8 = 30,000 bytes.

(*b*) There are two silhouettes per page so the total storage requirements

= 15,000 bytes × 2 × 120 = 3,600,000 bytes. **(1 mark)**

= 3,600,000/1,024 Kb = 3,516 Kb

= 3,516/1,024 = 3.43 Mb **(1 mark)**

HINT

It is a common mistake to use 1,000 instead of 1,024 when converting bytes into Kilobytes. Always use 1 Kilobyte = 1,024 bytes.

The following answer would still gain all two marks even though it is wrong! This is because the wrong answer from part (a) has been used as the basis of the calculation in part (b) but the calculation itself is correct.

There are two silhouettes per page so the total storage requirements

= 30,000 bytes × 2 × 120 = 7,200,000 bytes.

= 7,200,000/1,024 Kb = 7,031 Kb

= 7,031 / 1,024 = 6.87 Mb

= 7 Mb.

A wrong answer can still obtain some of the marks if the working is shown, because marks can be given for the steps that are correct even if the final answer is wrong. ALWAYS SHOW THE WORKING IN A QUESTION THAT INVOLVES CALCULATIONS.

(*c*) Cropping. **(1 mark)**

HINT

Don't confuse cropping with reducing a graphic. Cropping is used to display part of an image by trimming its edges but reducing simply makes the image smaller.

(*d*) (i) Desk top publishing is used to produce documents that combine text and graphics. The creation of the book requires text and graphics of the silhouettes to be placed alongside each other. (**1 mark**)

(ii) Text wrap can be used to make the text flow around the graphic instead of covering it up. (**1 mark**)

4. This question uses the College of Fine Arts setting to examine several topics across the syllabus. The topics include Hardware, Presentation and Multimedia and Operating Systems.

4. (*a*) Alice can use a scanner to scan the lecture notes into a computer (**1 mark**) and then use optical character recognition (OCR) software which turns it into editable text. (**1 mark**)

HINT It is important to state the hardware device (scanner) that is needed to input the documents into a computer system but equally that OCR software is required to recognise the characters as well.

(*b*) Thin Film Transistor. (**1 mark**)

(*c*) A USB flash memory stick / Possibly a CD-RW or DVD-RW. (**1 mark**)

HINT The key point here is that the file requires 12.3 Mb of storage so a floppy disk would not do (1.4 Mb). You should keep up to date with the current capacity of storage devices such as CD, DVD, USB flash, etc. to improve your answer to this type of question.

TOP EXAM TIP

You are expected to provide fuller and more detailed answers in a Credit paper than in a General paper. This is particularly important in PS questions, where an explanation or justification is required and not just the statement of a fact or a simple decryption as is expected in KU questions.

Many candidates fail to address the Credit paper at the depth required at this level.

(*d*) (i) An authoring package can be programmed to a greater extent than a presentation package. (**1 mark**)

An authoring package produces a stand-alone application but a presentation package requires the program used to create it to run it. (**1 mark**)

(ii) Hyperlinks can be used to create a link from one slide to any other slide. (**1 mark**)

HINT Hyperlinks are also used in webpages to provide links to other webpages and websites.

(*e*) (i) Hierarchical filing system. (**1 mark**)

HINT Older computers used a single level filing system where a disc displayed all of the files in a single directory and there were no sub directories. You are probably so used to a hierarchical filing system that you take it for granted!

(ii) Any **two** of the following answers would gain **1 mark** each:

Files can be grouped together in a logical manner so that it is easy to find files. (**1 mark**)

Files can have the same name provided that they are not in the same directory. (**1 mark**)

In a network, different directories can be given different access rights (read/write, read only etc.) to the network users. (**1 mark**)

5. This question uses a computerised chemical process to target the main points in the Credit exam on Industrial Applications and Automated Systems.

5. (*a*) A-Pressure sensor. (**1 mark**)

B-A to D converter. (**1 mark**)

C-Digital data. (**1 mark**)

Each of the labels A, B and C are clearly identified.

HINT You must make it clear which term goes with which label in this type of question.

(*b*) The analogue data has to be converted into digital data to be in a form that can be stored on a computer. (**1 mark**)

HINT A description of analogue and digital data can get quite philosophical. What you need to know here is that quantities such as temperature and pressure change smoothly (analogue data). A computer is digital and can't store infinitely small changes and so stores the changing data in small steps with tiny gaps between the values stored (digital data).

(*c*) The program in the ROM chip cannot be overwritten or deleted. (**1 mark**)

The program in the ROM chip does not lose its contents when the computer is switched off. (**1 mark**)

HINT These are the two main reasons why programs are stored in ROM and the answer is awarded 2 marks. A third reason could have been that there is no delay in loading the program at start-up since it is stored permanently in ROM.

(*d*) An embedded system is the hardware and software that forms part of a larger system.

HINT Embedded systems are asked for frequently in the exam but students often give an answer that is too vague or incomplete. Make sure that you learn the precise definition given in this answer.

6. This a typical Credit level spreadsheet question. The use of absolute/relative cell referencing and the IF function are covered again (See Credit Paper A, question 2) because of their importance in that they are nearly always asked for in the Credit exam.

6. (*a*) (i) Cell attributes are the ways in which the data can be displayed in a cell. eg. The number of decimal places, the way a date is displayed, currency, etc. (**1 mark**)

HINT Don't confuse cell attributes with cell formatting which is the appearance of the cell itself. i.e. The cell height, width, border thickness, fill pattern, etc.

(ii) The cell attributes of cells G2 to G6 can be altered to be displayed as currency. (**1 mark**) (*b*) (i) Replicated is when a formula is copied down or across a range of cells. **(1 mark)**

(ii) =$B$2*E2+$B$3*F2. **(2 marks)**

> **HINT** 1 mark is awarded for using the correct cells in the formula and 1 mark is awarded for indication that cells B2 and B3 have dollar signs to make them absolute cell references.

(*c*) A new row can be inserted between row 6 and row 7 and then the data for Saturday can be entered. **(1 mark)**

> **HINT** A lot of pupils answer this question by stating that the data in row 6 and row 7 should be cut and then pasted one row lower down. This technique would work but it is better to insert a row which requires fewer actions and is therefore more efficient.

(*d*) = IF (G7 >= 50, "Yes", "No"). **(3 marks)**

> **HINT** 1 mark is given for the IF function, 1 mark for the condition "G6 >= 50" and 1 mark for the text "No"

TOP EXAM TIP

PAST PAPERS

The content of the Standard Grade Computing Studies exam was updated in the summer of 2006 to take account of changes in computing. You should certainly get a copy of the past papers from 2006 onwards at both General and Credit level. Papers from 2007 are available for free via the SQA's website. Papers before this date are still partially relevant but a significant percentage of the content has been changed and can lead to confusion of what you should and should not know. A good idea would be to ask your teacher which questions are still worth doing in the papers before 2006.

Your own school may also be able to give you copies of the prelim exam used for previous years. These papers will be similar in style and content to what you can expect in the actual exam.

> **7.** This question covers the topic Expert Systems and the areas of virtual reality and wireless technologies. Three of the marks are allocated to giving advantages. It is important to write a sentence to give explanation in these answers and not to give answers such as "Neater.", "Quicker." or "Better.".

7. (*a*) Multi-user database. **(1 mark)**

(*b*) (i) Virtual reality is an interactive simulation of the real world on a computer system. **(1 mark)**

(ii) Any **two** of the following answers would gain **1 mark** each:

Training can take place in a safe environment.

Extreme or rare situations can be created.

Saving on costs of materials such as anesthetics.

No harm is done to the animals.

(*c*) (i) Any **one** of the following answers would gain **1 mark**:

Young women are suited to a poodle. **(1 mark)**

Men who play rugby are suited to an Alsatian. **(1 mark)**

People with a low income are suited to a dog that does not need much food. **(1 mark)**

> **HINT** This question has an almost infinite number of possible answers. The answers given here give an idea of a rule or fact that would gain a mark.

(ii) Any **one** of the following answers would gain **1 mark**:

A faster diagnosis than a human being could make. **(1 mark)**

There is a consistently accurate advice. **(1 mark)**

More facts and rules can be included in the knowledge base than a human could remember. **(1 mark)**

(*d*) (i) Bluetooth allows devices such as mobile phones and laptops to communicate with each other over a short distance using radio waves. **(1 mark)**

Wi-Fi allows equipped laptops with a wireless network interface card to access the Internet in areas called hotspots using radio waves. **(1 mark)**

(ii) Internet Service Provider. **(1 mark)**

HINT: Be careful with this type of question and make sure that your answer is precise. You will gain no marks for an answer such as "Internet Server Provider" or "Internet Service Provision".

8. This question covers aspects of the Low Level Machine topic. This area of the syllabus is covered less frequently in the exam than it used to be but can still make up a significant number of marks.

8. (*a*) Any **two** of the following answers would gain **1 mark** each:

Passwords can be used to restrict access to files. **(1 mark)**

Data can be encrypted (putting data into a code) **(1 mark)**

Physical methods such as locks on doors can be used. **(1 mark)**

(*b*) (i) RAM. **(1 mark)**

HINT: The program is loaded into RAM (Random Access Memory) since ROM (Read Only Memory) can't be written to.

(ii) Main memory is made up of millions of storage locations which hold program instructions and data. Each location is given a unique address so that the processor can identify it. **(1 mark)**

HINT: The concept of the processor being able to address individual storage locations is called **addressability**.

(*c*) A word. **(1 mark)**

HINT: The term word has a specific meaning in a processor. It is nothing to do with English words but describes a group of bits that are transferred as a unit within the processor.

(*d*) A graphics card is a circuit board that stores and processes the graphics on a computer system. **(1 mark)**

HINT: Graphics and sound cards perform a similar function. A graphics card stores and processes graphics data while sound card stores and processes sound data.

TOP EXAM TIP

EXAMINER'S REPORT

Each year, the SQA publish an examiner's report which details the strengths and weaknesses of the candidates in their performance in the Foundation, General and Credit exams.

It gives specific details on the questions in which students performed well but also details the areas which students found demanding.

There is also more general advice on how to prepare students better for future exams.

There is an examiner's report for the 2006, 2007 and 2008 exams.

The reports are freely available on-line at www.sqa.org.uk or you can probably get them from your teacher.

1. This question brings together several topics but mainly examines key points in the commercial data processing chapter.

1. (*a*) The formula to be entered into cell E2 is =C2+(D2*0.1) (**1 mark** for 'C2' and **1 mark** for '(D2*0.1)')

HINT: 1 mark should be taken off for each mistake in your answer. However, don't take off more than 2 marks since you are never given a negative mark for an answer in this course.

(*b*) Replication. (**1 mark**)

HINT: Fill down would also be accepted as an answer to this question but replication is the correct technical term and is a better answer.

(*c*) The cell attributes of these cells should be changed to currency. (**1 mark**)

(*d*) The data for Jamie in row 5 of the spreadsheet should be deleted. (**1 mark**)

HINT: When a row is deleted in a spreadsheet, the other rows close up so that there is no blank row left.

(*e*) (i) The data in rows A and E should be highlighted (**1 mark**) and then the bar chart option chosen from the charting menu. (**1 mark**)

(ii) A wizard. (**1 mark**)

(*f*) =AVERAGE(E2:E8) (**1 mark** for 'AVERAGE' and **1 mark** for '(E2:E8)')

HINT: Another possible answer here is =(E2+E3+E4+E5+E6+E7+E8)/7 but technically this is a formula and not a function and also it is less efficient than the AVERAGE function.

2. This question examines a mixture of knowledge and understanding and problem solving questions on the word processing topic.

2. (*a*) Word processing. (**1 mark**)

HINT: Word processing is required for this situation because it is text editing. A database is for storing and retrieving data and graphics packages are for editing images.

(*b*) (i) Footers. (**1 mark**)

(ii) Alice can insert page numbers into a footer which will automatically appear on every page in the document and save her time in typing them and keeping track of the numbers. (**1 mark**)

(*c*) The search and replace feature (**1 mark**) can be used to enter "Stephanie" for the text to be replaced and "Sophie" for the replacement text. (**1 mark**)

HINT It is a common mistake to say that each occurrence of Stephanie should be deleted and then Sophie typed in. This, of course, would work but it is certainly not efficient and would not gain any marks here. Note that simply stating 'Search = Stephanie, replace = Sophie' would be enough for the **2 marks**.

(*d*) Word-wrap is when a word becomes too long to fit at the end of a line and automatically goes down to the start of the next line. (**1 mark**)

HINT Don't mix up word-wrap with text-wrap which is where text flows around a graphic.

The page break feature moves the cursor to the start of the next page. (**1 mark**)

(*f*) (i) Alice can highlight the text on a page (**1 mark**) and then choose the word count option. (**1 mark**).

(ii) She can increase the font size of the text. (**1 mark**)

TOP EXAM TIP

When studying for the exam it is better to study in lots of short periods than in fewer long periods. Studies have shown that your studying will be more effective and that you will remember more.

HINT It is better to use the technical term font size than simply to state that the text should be made bigger.

She can increase the size of the page margins to allow less room for the text. (**1 mark**)

3. This question covers most aspects of the General content of the database topic but also brings in some of the legal issues of the course.

3. (*a*) (i) There are 5 fields in the database. (**1 mark**)

(ii) The Last Visit is a date field. (**1 mark**)

(iii) Any **one** of the following answers would gain **2 marks**:

Address field (**1 mark**) which is a text field. (**1 mark**)

Treatment history (**1 mark**) which is a text field. (**1 mark**)

Date of birth (**1 mark**) which is a date field. (**1 mark**)

Number of visits (**1 mark**) which is a numeric field. (**1 mark**)

HINT There is a virtually limitless number of answers to this question but try and think of a field that is useful in the context of the question.

(*b*) A complex sort has been performed with the *Treatment* (**1 mark**) field in *ascending* (**1 mark**) order and the *Age* (**1 mark**) field in *descending* (**1 mark**) order.

(*c*) They can keep a backup copy of the file on a disc or other suitable backing store device. (**1 mark**)

4. This question uses two types of exam question. One type asks you to state what the initials of a term stand for and the other asks you tick a box to indicate the correct answer. Both of these types of question are becoming more popular in the exam so prepare yourself for them.

4. (*a*) (i) Desk Top Publishing. (**1 mark**)

(ii) Video. (**1 mark**)

HINT: It is common for students to mix up the elements of DTP with multimedia systems. Text, graphics, video and sound are elements of multimedia but not DTP which is only text and graphics.

(*b*) A template is a document with some of the content and formatting already in place that can be used over and over again as the basis for a document. (**1 mark**)

(*c*) (i) Any **two** of the following answers would gain **1 mark** each:

The e-mail would arrive much quicker than by post. (**1 mark**)

The article would not need to be typed into the computer. (**1 mark**)

HINT: Other answers such as, "It might get lost in the post." are OK but the two answers given above are probably the best to ensure the two marks.

(ii) A disadvantage of e-mails is that they can be used to transfer viruses. (**1 mark**)

(*d*) (i) Any **two** of the following answers would gain **1 mark** each:

Creates, deletes and amends user accounts. (**1 mark**)

Installs new software. (**1 mark**)

Installs and maintains printers. (**1 mark**)

(ii) Any **two** of the following answers would gain **1 mark** each:

Writes computer programs. (**1 mark**)

Tests computer programs. (**1 mark**)

Maintains computer programs. (**1 mark**)

TOP EXAM TIP

It is important to know exactly what course content you need to know for the Standard Grade exams. Look up the details of the exam syllabus on the SQA website at www.sqa.org.uk.

5. This question has mainly **1 mark** questions on the integrated packages and graphics topics. In general you are only expected to make one point for a **1 mark** question.

5. (*a*) The attributes of the rectangle has been changed to make its border pattern dashed. (**1 mark**)

The text has been changed from italics text to plain. (**1 mark**)

(*b*) Binary codes for colours of pixels. (**1 mark**)

HINT: This is the best answer since it mentions that graphics are stored as codes for colour of pixels and not just binary numbers

(*c*) (i) An integrated package is a software package that has two or more general purpose packages in the one program. (**1 mark**)

(ii) The general purpose packages will have a common HCI, unlike an individual package where the HCI can be very different in each package and harder to learn. (**1 mark**)

(*d*) A toolbar is a group of related icons. (**1 mark**)

HINT — This sort of question requires a fairly precise definition. You will not get a mark for answering with something along the lines of "Pictures that you click on to help you." which is not clear enough in its explanation.

(*e*) Scaling. (**1 mark**)

HINT — Scaling a graphic is to enlarge or reduce it.

(*f*) (i) Any **one** of the following answers would gain a mark:

A laser printer prints faster than an inkjet printer. (**1 mark**)

A laser printer produces better quality printouts than an inkjet printer. (**1 mark**)

(ii) d.p.i. (dots per inch)

HINT — There are other possible answers here but the ones given above will certainly gain marks.

6. This question examines hardware devices. You are expected to know how to compare hardware devices in terms of characteristics such as speed and capacity, as well as what they are used for.

6. (*a*) A portable device could be USB flash, CD-R, CD-RW, DVD-R, DVD-RW, etc. (**1 mark**)

HINT — A floppy disk is still an acceptable answer but these are disappearing as higher capacity devices become cheaper and cheaper.

(*b*) (i) Keyboard, mouse, scanner, digital camera, digital camcorder, graphics tablet, joystick, etc. (**1 mark**)

(ii) Printer, monitor, graph plotter, etc. (**1 mark**)

HINT — There are many more answers to this question since there are dozens of input and output devices available for computers.

(*c*) (i) Random Access Memory. (**1 mark**)

(ii) Increasing the amount or RAM on a computer means that the computer can run larger programs and process larger data files such as video and sound. (**1 mark**)

(iii) ROM. (**1 mark**)

TOP EXAM TIP

It is sometimes a good idea to study with one or two friends. This way you can learn from each other's strengths and build confidence.

HINT — There is often a question on the components of main memory (RAM and ROM) in the exam.

(*d*) The program that manages the hardware of a computer system is called an operating system. (**1 mark**)

HINT — It is important to use the general term operating system to answer this question and not to give an example of a specific commercial operating system such as Windows which will not gain a mark.

(*e*) An expert system. (**1 mark**)

(*f*) World Wide Web. (**1 mark**)

7. This is a typical General level question on automated systems. This area of the course often asks for social issues of computing as well as technical issues.

7. (*a*) The workers might be concerned that they could lose their jobs due to the introduction of the robots. (**1 mark**)

(*b*) The initial costs are the cost of the robots themselves, the software to run the robots, the installation of safety barriers, etc. (**1 mark**)

The running costs are the maintenance of the robots, re-programming the robots, etc. (**1 mark**)

HINT Learn the difference between initial costs and running costs since they are frequently asked for in the exam.

(*c*) Any **two** of the following answers would gain **1 mark** each:

Safety barriers round machines. (**1 mark**)

Blinking lights on machines. (**1 mark**)

Warning sirens when people are in a dangerous position. (**1 mark**)

(*d*) The waist. (**1 mark**)

HINT The anatomy of a robot arm is the same as a human. It has a waist, shoulder, elbow and wrist.

(*e*) Any **two** of the following answers would gain **1 mark** each:

The robots can work 24/7. (**1 mark**)

Robots never go on strike. (**1 mark**)

The robots can work faster than humans. (**1 mark**)

8. This is the last question in this paper. You can normally expect to have 8 or 9 questions in the General exam but make sure that you do all the questions. Every year, students miss out some of the questions at the end of the paper by not checking that they have finished the exam.

8. (*a*) (i) Range check. (**1 mark**)

(ii) Errors can be detected by using a length check, which means that the program only accepts candidate numbers that are exactly 8 characters long. (**1 mark**)

(*b*) Real-time processing. (**1 mark**)

(*c*) The college would pay for the list so that they can send mailshots to try to attract potential students to the college. (**1 mark**)

HINT This question addresses the sale of customer lists by companies holding data. Watch out for this type of question as it has appeared a lot in past exams.

(*d*) Any **two** of the following answers would gain **1 mark** each:

A broadband connection is very fast. **(1 mark)**

The connection is always on. **(1 mark)**

A broadband connection can carry many different channels of data on one cable. **(1 mark)**

Can use the phone at the same time as using the Internet. **(1 mark)**

TOP EXAM TIP

The timetable for the SQA exams is published many months before the actual exams. Ask you teacher for a copy of this timetable. Knowing how many days you have between exams will allow you to plan your studying better.

1. This question covers commonly examined aspects of spreadsheets in the Credit exam. It is essential that you know about absolute and relative cell references and replication.

1. (*a*) (i) Cell B6 contains the formula =C6+D6+E6 (**1 mark**)

HINT It is important to put the "=" in front of a formula and not just C6+D6+E6. You could also have answered "=SUM(C6:E6)".

(ii) The cell references C6, D6 and E6 need to change for each row when the formula is replicated down column B. (**1 mark**)

(*b*) (i) An absolute cell reference is one which does not change when a formula is replicated. (**1 mark**)

(ii) The formula in cell F6 is =$B$2*C6+$B$3*D6 (**2 marks**)

HINT 1 mark is given for the correct formula and the second mark for correct use of absolute and relative cell references. The dollar signs around B2 and B3 are used to make them absolute cell references.

(*c*) (i) The Won and the Points columns would automatically increase for teams that had won at least one game. (**1 mark**)

(ii) A dynamic link means that the bar chart automatically changes when the data in the spreadsheet is changed. With a static link the graph would not change and would need to be repeatedly re-done every time the data changed.
(**1 mark**)

(*d*) An expert user can carry out tasks quicker than by using the mouse to choose from menus and icons. (**1 mark**)

(*e*) Rows 5 to 8 are highlighted (**1 mark**) and then PRINT is chosen from a menu.
(**1 mark**)

HINT To print out part of any document the section to be printed has to highlighted or specified in some way. Simply to say to print would not gain both marks in this question.

(*f*) (i) Cell protection. (**1 mark**)

(ii) Any cell from B6 to B15 or F6 to F15 or row 5. (**1 mark**)

HINT Any cell which contains a label or a formula that never changes can be locked.

2. This question covers the use of stationary robots in factory assembly lines. Other papers in this book cover the use of mobile robots.

2. (*a*) Any **one** of the following advantages would gain **1 mark**:

Paint spraying toys. (**1 mark**)

Welding parts together. (**1 mark**)

Moving parts into position. (**1 mark**)

HINT

There are a variety of answers to this question but the ones given above will gain the marks. Be careful not too stray to far away from basics in this type of question and give an answer such as "Load the toys onto aeroplanes."

(*b*) Adaptable means that the robot is flexible in that it can change what it does to respond to changes in its environment. (**1 mark**)

(*c*) Any **two** of the following answers would gain **1 mark** each:

There would be less need for eating and toilet facility. (**1 mark**)

There would be less heating and lighting required. (**1 mark**)

Safety measures such as barriers around the robots would be installed. (**1 mark**)

(*d*) (i) A control language has commands and features that are specifically suited to writing a program to instruct a robot to perform a task. (**1 mark**)

HINT

It is quite common to be asked about control languages in the exam. Students often answer this question badly so study this question and the answer.

TOP EXAM TIP

Lay out your equipment you require for the exam the day before. You don't want to be rushing in the morning of the exam to find a pen or pencil. Make sure that you have pens, pencils, ruler, rubber, sharpener and a working calculator.

(ii) A compiled program runs relatively fast since no translation is required when the program is run. (**1 mark**)

Once the program has been compiled, the source code and the programming language are no longer required to run the program, therefore it will use less memory. (**1 mark**)

(iii) Any **two** of the following answers would gain **1 mark** each:

The program is always in ROM and there is no waiting time to load it up. (**1 mark**)

The contents of ROM can't be deliberately or accidentally changed. (**1 mark**)

A ROM chip keeps its contents when the power is switched off. (**1 mark**)

(*e*) An A to D converter is required because heat from the temperature sensors is analogue data which must be converted to digital data to be entered into a computer. (**1 mark**)

HINT

Usually A to D converters are examined in the Credit exam as opposed to D to A converters. D to A converters are used when a computer outputs data to an analogue device such as an electric motor.

3. This question covers the input of data into a computer system through OMR and OCR. It is important that you know how to describe these methods of data input and their advantages and disadvantages.

3. (*a*) The document is called a mark sense card. **(1 mark)**

HINT: It is a common mistake to call this document OMR (Optical Mark Recognition). Remember that OMR is the name of the process of inputting data, the document itself is called a mark sense card.

(*b*) It is relatively simple for a computer to recognise the position of a mark but Optical Character Recognition requires the shapes of characters to be identified. Messy or incomplete handwriting can cause errors. **(1 mark)**

(*c*) (i) Mainframe. **(1 mark)**

(ii) A mainframe is an expensive powerful computer which is required to store and process the vast amount of data held in the lottery tickets. **(1 mark)**

(*d*) (i) The storage requirements of all the tickets

= 64 bytes × 48,000,000

= 3,072,000,000 bytes **(1 mark)**

= 3,072,000,000/1,048,576 Megabytes

= 2,930 Megabytes. **(1 mark)**

HINT: To convert bytes into Mb can be done in one step by dividing by 1,048,576. If you find it hard to remember the number of bytes in a Mb then you can divide by 1,024 to convert bytes to Kb and then by 1,024 again to get Mb.

(ii) A hard disk **(1 mark)** because it has a large capacity to store all the data week after week and it also has fast direct/random access which is required to quickly load the data. **(1 mark)**

4. This question involves the calculation of the capacity of a black and white graphic from its dimension in pixels. This is a common question and an easy gift of marks, provided that you learn the steps of the calculation given here.

4. (*a*) The graphic has 1,200 × 1,280 = 1,536,000 pixels.

Each pixel requires 1 bit of storage = 1,536,000 bits. **(1 mark)**

1,536,000/8 = 192,000 bytes = 192,000/1024 = 187.5 Kb. **(1 mark)**

(*b*) (i) GIF (Graphics Interchange Format) **(1 mark)**

JPEG (Joint Photographic Experts Group) **(1 mark)**

HINT: There are other standard file formats for graphics such as TIFF but GIF and JPEG are very commonly used and well known.

(ii) A file saved in a standard file format will be able to be opened by other graphics programs apart from the one used to create it. **(1 mark)**

TOP EXAM TIP

Don't leave all your studying to the last minute. The night before the exam you should be relaxing and remaining calm and not in a panic to study things that you could have looked at weeks ago.

(*c*) Cropping means to trim the horizontal and vertical edges of a graphic. **(1 mark)**

HINT It is a common mistake to confuse cropping with scaling. Reducing a graphic by scaling means to make the graphic smaller but not to cut bits off.

(*d*) (i) Desk Top Publishing (DTP). **(1 mark)**

(ii) Any **two** of the following answers would gain **1 mark** each:

Changes can be made to the content of menus and toolbars. **(1 mark)**
The colour scheme, the font size used in menus and dialogue boxes can be altered. **(1 mark)**

The size and pictures in icons can be changed. **(1 mark)**

HINT There is an endless list of answers to this question but the ones given above are certainly good for gaining the marks.

5. You will not be asked about client/server networks and network interface cards in the General exam. It is frequently answered poorly in the Credit exam, so study this typical question given below and the answers.

5. (*a*) (i) A client/server network is a LAN where server computers provide network resources **(1 mark)** that are accessed by network users on client computers. **(1 mark)**

(ii) File server. **(1 mark)**

Print server. **(1 mark)**

HINT There are other servers, such as a web server, and a multimedia server, but a file and print server are probably the best answers to give as they are essential on most networks.

(iii) Network Interface Card (NIC). **(1 mark)**

(*b*) A complex search is made where the Species field = "Elephant" **(1 mark)** AND the Age field < 10. **(1 mark)**

(*c*) The process is called mail merge. **(1 mark)**

(*d*) (i) A WYSIWYG editor allows the elements of the web page to be simply dragged and dropped onto the page but using HTML would require a lot of technical knowledge of this language and be much more time consuming. **(1 mark)**

(ii) Audio and video can be included by creating a hyperlink to the audio or video file **(1 mark)** or by embedding the file in the web page. **(1 mark)**

(*e*) Any **two** of the following answers would gain **1 mark** each:

An expert system makes a faster diagnosis than a human. **(1 mark)**

There is a more consistently accurate diagnosis than a human. **(1 mark)**

Rare cases can be included in the knowledge base that might not be known by a human. **(1 mark)**

There is cost savings by removing the need to pay a human expert. **(1 mark)**

(*f*) (i) Electronic Funds Transfer **(1 mark)**

HINT Also watch out for the term EFTPOS (Electronic Funds Transfer at Point Of Sale).

(ii) Any **two** of the following answers would gain **1 mark** each:

EFT removes the need to carry money. (**1 mark**)

It is more secure than paying for goods by cash. (**1 mark**)

Time is saved in counting money. (**1 mark**)

There is no need to go to a bank to withdraw and deposit money. (**1 mark**)

(*g*) (i) The computers can be moved around freely since they don't need to be connected to a specific point (**1 mark**) and there is a safer, less cluttered environment in the workplace. (**1 mark**)

(ii) Palmtop / laptop / mobile phone (**2 marks**)

6. This question covers the hardware and software areas of the syllabus. It is important that you know about different types of computers (desktop, laptop, palmtop) and their input, output and backing store devices.

6. (*a*) (i) Multimedia is a computer system that displays text, graphics, video and sound in an interactive environment. (**1 mark**)

(ii) The PowerPlusII Desktop is best suited to Polly's needs (**1 mark**) because it has a faster processor and more memory than the Total D2000 Laptop, which is required to manage the large files involved in multimedia programs. (**1 mark**)

(*b*) The desktop computer has a re-writeable DVD disk drive that can be used to backup data but the laptop has a CD ROM drive that can't be written to. (**1 mark**)

(*c*) A hard disk has direct access. (**1 mark**)

HINT Direct access is also known as random access which is an equally acceptable answer to this question.

(*d*) Any **two** of the following answers would gain **1 mark** each:

The operating system provides a Human Computer Interface (HCI) for the user. (**1 mark**)

File Management controls the saving and loading of files on disk. (**1 mark**)

Memory Management controls where program and data files are loaded into main memory. (**1 mark**)

Input/Output controls the reading of data from input devices and the sending of data to output devices. (**1 mark**)

Process Management controls the allocation of the processor time when it is shared between two or more tasks. (**1 mark**)

Error Reporting lets the user know if any mistakes have occurred. (**1 mark**)

HINT — There are several answers provided for this question because the standard functions of an operating system come up frequently in the exam.

(*e*) Thin Film Transistor. **(1 mark)**

7. This is the last question in the book so I will not describe the question but take the opportunity to wish you good luck in the exam.

7. (*a*) Virtual reality is a method of simulating the real world in a computer system. **(1 mark)**

(*b*) Any **two** of the following answers would gain **1 mark** each:

There is less chance of a skier being injured. **(1 mark)**

Time and money is saved in travelling and lodging at a ski resort. **(1 mark)**

Challenging runs and snow conditions can be created. **(1 mark)**

HINT — It is important to give an answer that is to the point in this kind of question. An answer such as "There is less chance of losing your keys in the snow." would probably not gain a mark.

(*c*) A systems analyst observes and analyses a system. **(1 mark)**

He advises upon which hardware and software is required to implement a computerised system. **(1 mark)**

(*d*) (i) The Data Protection Act (1984). **(1 mark)**

(ii) Any **one** of the following requirements would gain **1 mark**:

A company wishing to hold data must register with a central government agency. **(1 mark)**

Data must be made secure by restricting access with passwords. **(1 mark)**

Data must be up to date and accurate. **(1 mark)**

Individuals have the right to demand a printout of their data. (Except for the Police.) **(1 mark)**

TOP EXAM TIP

There are revision books available for Standard Grade Computing. These are a very useful way to revise for the exam since they give a short but full coverage of the course in a more manageable form than a full blown textbook. You can find these on the Leckie and Leckie website (www.leckieandleckie.co.uk)